WHEN WALLS
BECOME BRIDGES

WHEN WALLS BECOME BRIDGES

A Journey of Discovery to Heal and Conquer Hatred

STUART LEWIS

Copyright © 2019 by
Stuart Lewis

All rights reserved.

Original Cover Art by Ashley Gould
Cover Layout by David Moratto
Translation of Frank's final letter from German by
Jonathan Styles, Berlin

First edition published in 2017.
Limited Editions Printed in Canada by Printing Icon.

Editing and Book Development Provided By
The Awakened Press
www.theawakenedpress.com

All rights reserved.

No part of this publication may be reproduced, stored in a retrieval system, or transmitted in any form by any means, electronic, mechanical, photocopying, recording, or otherwise, without written permission from the publisher. The only exception is brief quotations in reviews and printed reviews written for inclusion in a magazine, newspaper or broadcast.

The addresses, email addresses and phone numbers in this book are accurate at the time of publication. They are provided as a resource. The publisher does not endorse them or vouch for their content or permanence.

Second edition.

ISBN: 978-1-989134-07-8

This work depicts actual events in my life as truthfully as recollection permits and/or can be verified by research. I have been corrected on some points, mostly of chronology. And on my dear friend and central figure Frank, his English, which is his second or third language, may in fact be better than mine—the evidence is here in the letters for the readers to determine for themselves.

I've allowed some of these points to remain as they are because this is a book from memory, and memory has its own perspective to tell. I understand that truth is subjective in nature, but I have done my best to make this a truthful story.

Occasionally, dialogue consistent with the character or nature of the event has been supplemented by my own memory of the situation. Although all persons mentioned within are actual individuals, some of their names have been changed to respect their privacy. I've also had some of the letters edited for grammatical purposes or privacy reasons while doing my best to exhibit them in their original form.

I would like to express my gratitude to the real life friends, acquaintances and members of the family portrayed. This book was not intended to hurt anyone, especially not the family. I realize that their memories of the events described may be different than my own. In fact, my hope and intention in regards to this work is that our walls will dismantle, or at least begin to, and that we can build a bridge that will continue to bring us closer together. As for myself and those involved in making this book happen, we regret any unintentional harm resulting from the publishing and marketing of When Walls Become Bridges: A Journey of Discovery to Heal and Conquer Hatred.

To my dear children—I love you all so deeply. The world is now in your hands…

Who knew?

The manifestation of love and gratitude is all I could think of as I wrote this section.

For my very being and every breath I take, I am now and will forever be indebted to my mother whom I love dearly.

To my beautiful, talented and extraordinary children, I am so privileged and honoured to be your father. I will hold that precious to me for as long as I live. And to their mother, I have respect and admiration for all you have done and continue to do for them.

My one and only brother has stood by me in ways I would never have thought possible. This book would not have been conceivable without you and your support. And to my sister—who actually came into my life when we were both adults—your emergence has been a blessing. You have provided unconditional love to me ever since.

Embarking on the undertaking of writing this book were so many people who have helped along the way. No contribution large or small was insignificant. There is Jonathan, Jeff, Fiona, Beth, Peter, Tim, Michael, Ashley, Greg, Dusan, Aruna, Suzanne, Kim, and David; and by unintentional omission, others I have surely failed to mention. David, an armed forces veteran, I have to single out for visiting my dad in the hospital ten days before his passing. That was an extraordinary encounter to witness. I felt like a fly on the wall watching the two of them "talk shop".

Finding my editor, Lindsay R. Allison, was the best stroke of luck this novice writer could have ever hoped to achieve. She saw the potential of my story from the outset and helped me immensely. Her expert and well-placed guidance, questions and probes were exactly what the book needed at the right time.

Kevin has been a dear and impactful friend of mine ever since university, although we attended different institutions. When I re-discovered the letters from Frank, Kevin and I met for beers one night. I had this brilliant idea that I would use the letters as inspiration and contextual reference towards writing a Cold War, espionage-packed spy thriller. Kevin looked at me with a sincere but stern, fatherly-like glance, and strongly suggested that the idea of writing fiction was not the best option for me to take with these letters. He then asked me a simple question that set this all in motion. "Do you know if Frank saved your letters?" Always the consummate journalist!

Dr. Izzeldin Abuelaish was an unexpected and magnificent gift to my soul. In so many ways, he was the catalyst towards setting me free. His inspiration, support and friendship is cherished and honoured.

Suzanne is one of the most exquisite humans I have ever met. She came into my life and this story at the perfect time and I am grateful to her for that.

I often try to imagine: what if I never went to East Berlin? Or, what if it had become just another cool place to have visited on that trip, just as the Eiffel Tower, the Coliseum or the race track of the Grand Prix of Monte Carlo? But I met Frank there. And that encounter was ultimately the genesis of this story.

To all the others who have journeyed with me these past several years, thank you for listening, for being there, for your reassurance, friendship and your love.

Where we go from here isn't as important as understanding how we got here and how high we have climbed.

—Stuart Lewis

CONTENTS

Prologue   A Window Into My World xvii

PART I
WHOSE WAR IS IT, ANYWAY?

Chapter 1	It Started With A Wall 1
Chapter 2	Détente 19
Chapter 3	Formed By The Past 31
Chapter 4	Home But Not Home 45
Chapter 5	Rituals 59
Chapter 6	German Knives 79
Chapter 7	Us Vs. Them 95
Chapter 8	The Berlin Wall Falls 123
Chapter 9	The Boil 145
Chapter 10	Rituals Take Hold 181
Chapter 11	My Earthquake 197

PART II
THE ENEMY WITHIN

Chapter 12	My Walls Crumble 209
Chapter 13	What Did My Father Do In The War? 229
Chapter 14	The War Hero 247
Epilogue	Who Is The Real Enemy? 251
Afterword	Denouement 255
Postscript	A Friendship Beyond Borders 257
Appendices 295
About The Author 301

WHEN WALLS
BECOME BRIDGES

PROLOGUE

A WINDOW INTO MY WORLD

> Man is the only animal for whom his own existence is a problem which he has to solve.
> —Erich Fromm

How is everything at home? I'm working as hard as I can to be with you as soon as I can. I'm keeping well, and I feel quite strong. I've got to be well, for I have so much to do for you all. I would like to know how Mummy is, as I miss her just as I miss you. Whatever happens, you will always be my family.
—Roy Lewis to his son Stuart, 1974

Because no matter what you've done, or what has happened, you will always be my father, and I love you for that.
—Stuart Lewis to his father, 1978

Hate is like a muscle: the more it is exercised, the stronger it becomes, and the more routine. We hate without even realizing it. What I am also referring to is everyday below the surface hate—the kind of hate we don't even think about.

Not a day goes by where there isn't yet another horrible report from somewhere to remind us of just how much hate animates our lives. It's relentless. A gunman walks into a mosque killing six worshippers in Quebec for no other reason other than the alleged "killer hated" Muslims.[1] A Jewish cemetery in a St. Louis suburb holds over one hundred headstones vandalized in an evening rampage.[2] A self-admitted white supremacist enters a Charleston, South Carolina church killing nine black parishioners.[3] In Canada, according to a CBC Marketplace study, there was a likely 600 percent increase from November 2015 to November 2016 in the amount of online language labelled as "racist, Islamophobic, sexist or otherwise intolerant."[4]

It seems endless and rather incomprehensible. We are overwhelmed both with impotent rage and soul-numbing fatigue. *What is going on? What is wrong with "these people"? Have they no decency? What is the point? When will it end?*

And then we forget. Until the next time.

* * * *

I never used to think of myself as someone who hates. And either at some point or at this time in your life, my guess is that neither do you. After all, now in the 21st century are we not all a more accepting and tolerant people?

In fact, I highly considered myself quite the opposite of a hater. For a very important and formative period of my life, I lived and embraced a religious lifestyle that preached acceptance, tolerance and forgiveness. In our attempt to be godlike and observant to God's commandments, how can one be hateful? Sure, I had my angry moments. Who doesn't? But hateful? No.

What I came to realize was that in many areas of my life where it mattered most, I was neither tolerant nor accepting or godlike—and certainly not forgiving.

Hate can be obvious. It may be walking into a shop and seeing a huge swastika flag draped across the back wall. It can be a sign on a beach declaiming, "No Dogs or Jews Allowed" (a very common sight in Toronto well into the 1950s).

But *hate* or intolerance or suspicion can also be a subtle and passive power in our lives. How? It can sometimes take the shape of benign respectability. It can be an article you read in the paper or see on TV about racial violence in some American city, or a bathroom access debate causing cries of discrimination based on sexual orientation from the LGBTQ community.

It may only take a second, but *there it is*…that familiar pronoun that just pops unbidden into your mind: *them*.

It can be that strange feeling you have when you see a woman wearing a hijab walk onto an airplane and the word *terrorist* comes to your mind. A homeless person can walk up to you and you assume he's a thief. It can be a man speaking German on a subway car and you think, *Nazi*.

Without meaning to, a wall goes up.

PART I

WHOSE WAR IS IT, ANYWAY?

CHAPTER 1

IT STARTED WITH A WALL

> One of the most beneficial and valuable gifts we can give to ourselves in this life: is allowing ourselves to be surprised! It is okay if life surprises you. It's a good thing!
> —C. JoyBell C.

Frank, I have great difficulty in categorizing you and I as "us" and "them". It is a sickening reality that is created by governments, not by people like you and me. It makes me wonder what those people in government are made of. Are they different from us in some way? I have the answer! If we could get a few hundred million people—half from the USA and NATO and half from the USSR and Warsaw Pact nations—to write letters to each other as we do, and then arrange an exchange of these people for a week or so…

That's it! All we need now is organization. Do you suppose that the UN could be put to some good use? Think about it. It could mean a joint Nobel Peace Prize for us.…

—Letter to Frank from Stuart, August 17, 1986

The most important friendships in our lives are often the most improbable, like the friendship between a German and a Jew.

I was raised utterly secular in Toronto, born to Jewish parents. At a point in my adult life, however, I embraced an orthodox religious lifestyle. Suddenly, I felt an adrenaline rush sense of meaning and belonging. The community of the like-minded—its rituals and rules and prescribed behaviours—seemed an effective antidote to doubt uncertainty and rootlessness. I committed myself; I embraced it and the cause with zealous passion.

And then, over a period of time, I realized that the solid footing beneath me was very slowly giving way. I have heard it said that people leave religion when they realize they have stopped believing. I have not stopped believing. It was more like a numbness had stilled the passion. The rituals that had seemed so vital to me suddenly seemed less of a means to an end than the end itself. Ritual was all there was. What for years had been as comfortable and necessary as breathing had become more and more of a laboured effort, not only an effort lacking in necessity, but losing…meaning.

Rabbi Jonathan Sacks wrote that "meaning is made, not just discovered."[5]

That is what religion for the most part is: the constant making and remaking of meaning, by the stories we tell, the rituals we perform and the prayers we believe we say. The stories are sacred, the rituals divine commands, and prayer an assumed dialogue with the divine. Religion is an authentic response to a real presence, but it is also a way of making that presence real by constantly living in response to it. It is truth translated into deed.

I once believed religion to be the truth. My orthodoxy had been a way for me to make meaning in my life—as a husband, as a father, as a Jew and as a person.

Meaning must be made, not discovered. But what is the *meaning* of meaning? I no longer knew; I wasn't even sure if I had ever known.

I felt like a composer suddenly deaf to the music he had created. I sensed I was waving my arms about, but had lost all interest in what those complicated and detailed gestures conveyed.

I was not making meaning, not anymore. And I wondered about those I observed surrounding me. Had belief metastasized in them into nothing but ritual? Nothing but a dull habit?

Forget about what this was doing in terms of making me a better and more devout Jew. Was any of this making me a more compassionate and decent human being? Not only did I carry a lingering bitterness towards Germans at the time, but also brewing inside of me were increasingly hostile feelings for the Arabs, Muslims and the Palestinian people. Was this making me a better person?

I didn't know, or maybe I did not want to know.

* * * *

We *can* change the world—at least each of us our own little part of the world—for the better, but not if we cannot commit to making change within ourselves. And the change we are able to make can be best achieved from the bottom up and not from the top down. We don't need extraordinary leaders or lesser ones; we have been there, done that, and for the most part they all have failed miserably. What is required of us is that *we* be extraordinary.

We ask ourselves, *"Why isn't something being done? Why don't THEY do something?"* Those questions lead us astray. "Why aren't *I* doing something? Why don't *we* do something?" are the questions that give the most meaning and produce the most outstanding results. In a world filled with hate and intolerance, bigotry and anger, I proved to myself that I can make a difference and that I could indeed change. So can we all.

I still believe that rituals guide us in making meaning in our lives. But sometimes rituals become an excuse to promulgate through repetitive performance and exalted emotions, even prejudice and hatred. We stop *making* meaning, and settle for dull comforts of recycling meaning. For as Rabbi Sacks wrote, it is not merely a process of making meaning but of *re-making* meaning. When we think we know what the truth is, we stop searching; we must have the courage at that point to continue on that quest.[6]

Rituals can be walls that we build up around ourselves (or around our tribe), usually as a defence against a threat. A wall can be a necessary act of self-preservation. However, a wall can also have the opposite effect: it can create a threat—or the *impression of a threat*. The impression created is that conflict—generally irresolvable conflict—is the only permissible outcome of our efforts to communicate with one another where ideological differences are present.

Conflict is not inevitable and differences cannot be ignored; they can be overcome. First, however, we need to find a new and more accommodating discourse in which to frame our disputes. Pitting one group against another, one person against another person, fostering an *Us vs. Them* environment only creates disunity, more walls and more seeds for the growth of potential conflict forever into the future.

Walls have taken me on a strange journey and down emotional roads that I never dreamed I would travel. A wall is an invitation to define those inside as "us" and those on the other side as "them".

I am more interested in bridges.

* * * *

My first encounter with a wall was very much emblematic of a historical confrontation. When I arrived in Berlin, I had already been travelling through Europe for a month and a half. I was in Hamburg the previous night and had a few pints at a local pub. When I boarded the train the next morning I noticed, somewhat blearily, something odd and very disconcerting: there were bars on the doors and windows of the train.

It was a real shock. In fact, when I reached the East German border, the civilian West German crew on the train had been replaced by uniformed East German guards with guns.

I was on alert. Somewhere deep in my mind I thought, *I am a Jew sitting on a train entering East Germany.*

Only a couple of weeks prior I had visited the notorious concentration camp at Dachau—the images of the Jewish people on a train in Germany haunted me, and it was extremely powerful.

I pushed the idea from my mind. *I had nothing to worry about. All that was ancient history.*

The guards changed over, and as my fellow travellers and I were sitting in a compartment we were all waiting to have our passports checked. It turned out that one of the travellers, who was American, couldn't find his passport. I will never forget that moment. The Communist guard entered, and the American man tried to explain that he must have lost it. I was sitting there, not knowing what the hell to do. A couple more guards showed up. One guard abruptly barked, *"Come with me,"* in heavily accented English, and the kid gathered up his backpack and they escorted him away from us.

A chill ran down my spine as I watched him being led away and remained in my bones later as the train chugged on, assuming our friend was left behind. To make ourselves feel at ease, we all agreed that most likely a call would be made to the American Embassy and it would all be straightened out, and it would make a hilarious story for him—one day. I wasn't really thinking that he had been tossed down a dark hole in the ground, but we all had that Cold War mindset: there was West Germany and there was East Germany, and the two political worlds were miles apart.

Yet, we were living the tension of the two Germanies in real time. It wasn't really in the faces of the people; the guards, for instance, were strict, but they seemed at ease for all the formality. It was more the atmosphere. It was a *sense*. The bars on the windows reinforced it, too.

The rest of the train ride was mostly pleasant, but redundant countryside led us all the way. This was a dedicated route and I wondered if the authorities designed it so the trains would not pass through any cities.

Travelling along I saw a soccer pitch where I noticed a worker cutting the grass with an old rotary mower. It was just this one poor guy with a mower and this regulation-sized soccer pitch. You could only imagine that by the time the labourer finished, he would have to start right up again in this seemingly never-ending cycle.

It was amazing.

That was probably my first reinforced preconception I had of a communist country. Like, who cuts the grass of a football field with a hand-push rotary mower—even in 1983? One of my unworldly expectations was of a very backward society, and this categorically confirmed my assumption.

As the train approached the outskirts of Berlin, it stopped and there was that exchange or switching of guards one last time. Then the train started up again, and off we went. At one point the train proceeded underground. Very shortly thereafter we disembarked in West Berlin.

At an information kiosk in the West Berlin underground portion of the train station of *Friedrichstrasse*, I met another American man, Hank, who was also at the kiosk looking for a room at a pension hotel. Like me, Hank had a university background in political science and both of us talked about how exciting it was to be in Berlin. It felt as though we were *living history* and not just reading about it. We talked about what brought us to Berlin, and we both concurred that we could not come all the way to Europe and not make the detour into East Berlin, despite the unbudgeted cost on top of our Eurail passes.

We successfully found an inexpensive room, checked in and dumped our gear there. We spent most of the day simply walking around the extraordinary city of West Berlin.

There was nothing like it. A notional island of a city altogether contained by a wall in another city of a vastly contradictory political system. The Wall was covered with an inordinate amount of mostly politically motivated graffiti.

That evening, Hank and I headed out to a bar and had some drinks. I was approached by a very attractive woman who wanted "to talk." *I like talking to pretty girls,* I thought. At one point she asked me if I wanted to buy her a drink. I tentatively agreed and then nearly fainted at discovering how much it cost—about all I had on me. It was only then that I realized it wasn't "talk" she was offering. Talk about being naïve.

Welcome to West Berlin!

The next morning, we woke up and walked the short distance from the pension and arrived at Checkpoint Charlie. It was surreal. Even now, I can hardly believe I was there. It felt so strange.

I will never forget the date.

June 11, 1983.

✷ ✷ ✷ ✷

East Berlin was a scene ripped directly from the pages of John le Carré's *The Spy Who Came in from the Cold*. Suddenly, it was as though the world had turned cinematic black and white; it was a complete contrast to what we had seen and experienced in West Berlin the day and night before.

Visiting East Berlin had never been my intention when originally planning my trip. In fact, being Jewish it was about the furthest thing from my mind. Most Westerners, myself included, who had grown up in the long shadow of the

Cold War had just assumed entry into East Berlin would be exceedingly problematic. I was genuinely surprised when a newfound friend in Garmisch-Partenkirchen mentioned how easy it was. For a day pass entry one didn't even need to apply in advance to obtain a visa. Apparently and quite accurately, I was told all one had to do was show up at Checkpoint Charlie with a valid passport and that was it.

At the time there was also the addition of a steep "entry fee". Well, at least for a student on a very tight daily budget, it was—and the exchange rate was awful, as one was forced to exchange West German marks for an "equal" of East German marks. Having already squandered a big chunk of my limited discretionary funds on the journey to Berlin, I was a bit nervous. This era was pre-ATM and I had no idea what might be involved with accessing cash "over there" in an East German bank, and the last thing I wanted was to end up penniless in East Berlin.

In addition to a passport, a visitor was issued what was called a *Tagesvisum*—a distinct document that functioned as a visa. It allowed one into East Berlin; it had to be surrendered upon entry back into West Berlin. This also served as a measure preventing those in East Berlin from escaping into the West through Checkpoint Charlie.

A secondary source of my fear going into East Berlin was that my passport had a recent Israeli visa stamp. At that time the Warsaw Pact countries were not overly welcoming to Israel, to say the least; they were allied with the Arab nations. And it had only been nine years since the Yom Kippur War. We were not talking ancient history. I kept telling myself it would be fine.

As I stood in the waiting room to have my entry processed, I had already been in line for about twenty minutes when I noticed an old and very religious Jewish gentleman standing ahead of me. He was visibly ultra-orthodox because of his thoroughly black attire, hat, long white beard; the full monty. His presence made me a bit more comfortable.

When it was my turn, I handed off my passport and exchanged the marks with the border official. As he took my passport behind a glass barrier, I was ushered into another room to wait. It was the first time in my life I had to relinquish my passport. Usually, you just flash your passport to a border agent and he says, "Thank you," and off you go. This was so much different. Without my passport in hand I felt the disorientation of losing my identity and of being temporarily stateless in a setting where I already had an uneasy feeling.

I waited for twenty minutes. Hank followed just behind me. We had no tangible reason to worry, but we did anyway. Hank was not Jewish, nor had he recently visited Israel. I felt uncomfortably vulnerable and exposed. If any of these East German guards decided they wanted to screw me over, they could. What could I have done?

But shortly after, my name was called and I got my passport back and received my Tagesvisum.

We were all searched before entering East Berlin. They went through my bag. No newspapers allowed. I had to surrender my *Time* magazine. I thought, *Wow, how do the East German people know anything about what is going on in the world if certain news is hidden from them? Were they aware of fake news?*

Vastly relieved, Hank and I entered East Berlin together. By that time we had met yet another American traveller, Jack, who asked if he could tag along. Why not? The more the merrier.

My first impressions of East Berlin were of pervasive and unrelieved industrial greyness. There were fully blossomed trees and a blue sky, as it was a perfect summer day, after all. But East Berlin looked to me like a bleak, cheerlessly concrete and mostly bombed-out relic.

The scenery was absolutely nothing new or fresh to my eyes—with one exception. Once a cattle market and military parade ground, the area—now known as Alexanderplatz—had been turned into a public square (renamed in honour of Tsar Alexander I on his visit to Berlin in 1805). During the regime of East German leader Erich Honecker in the 1970s, Alexanderplatz had been once more redeveloped and expanded as a modern socialist experiment. Even it, however, was looking a bit shabby.

Otherwise, East Berlin looked weary and a bit hungover; run-down and second or thirdhand. Along entire blocks of the city, remnants of bullet holes as large as a fist and strafing across walls could still be easily discerned. If there had been any other civic improvements, they were well hidden.

For someone like me from the West, the lack of abundant modern conveniences and shops was palpable. Stores in East Berlin were a caricature of what I was familiar with in the West.

I had never appreciated how much "stuff" we had back home, and was almost embarrassed by our abundance.

I have a photo of Hank standing beside a Trabant—a tiny utilitarian car the East Germans produced. We looked inside, and there was nothing visible but a steering wheel. I don't even think there was a speedometer, but there must have been at least that. You can't imagine. It wasn't as bad as Fred Flintstone's Stone Age car with Fred having to propel it with his feet to make the car move, but it was a close second.

We walked around for a couple of hours taking in the sites until the three of us ended up in a quaint outdoor café. It was a very nice day, sunny and warm. It turned out that Jack was hell-bent to meet "a real live Commie." His words. His accent denoted he originated from the American South. I remember my nervous laughter at what he was up to. Hank laughed, too, and said, "Go for it." Truth is, I think we both thought he was bluffing. But Jack stood up, and Hank and I watched in amazement as he walked across the courtyard and stopped at a table where two guys roughly our age were sitting. They talked ever so briefly, and the next thing we knew Jack was leading them back to our table.

He introduced us to "the two Franks."

Both Franks spoke English, but one was more fluent; and so naturally, he did most of the talking. From then on I secretly—to myself—named the more fluent speaker as "my Frank" and his friend "the other Frank". They were classmates in medical school in East Berlin and had learned English mostly from having to read medical textbooks that were in English. Their second language learned in school was Russian.

The five of us spent just over two hours talking and sightseeing.

I'll be honest: I was pretty impressed with myself. I graduated with a degree in political science and economics from the politically astute Carleton University in Ottawa,

Canada's capital city. I felt I had a fairly sophisticated and enlightened command of the world and geopolitics and how they interacted (or didn't, as was more often the case).

I was the "smart Canadian" with the political intellect and the confiscated *Time* magazine—and how lucky for the two Franks that I was there to educate them about the world!

Along the way we decided to stop and have a beer. As the discussion turned to a possible crack in the Warsaw Pact, in my naïveté I thought I would inform the Franks about the Solidarity movement in Poland. I talked about Lech Walesa and the shipyard workers he represented and their fight for freedom and human rights. I began to tell them all that was going on regarding the latest developments, and then my Frank gave me a frozen look that stopped me cold and said:

"Where do you think you are?"

I kind of sat back. I was stunned. So I said, "Communist Germany. I know where I am."

He asked me, "What is on the other side of the Wall?"

Wow. Okay, so based on my previous night in West Berlin, I thought I knew the answer he was looking for. On the other side of the Wall, I saw opulence and affluence, fancy cars and extremely expensive prostitutes. West Berlin appeared as a thriving, colourful, fully modern and exciting city like New York or London. I started to tell Frank about my experiences—how my bag was searched, newspapers confiscated and all that, and he just said, "Stop."

I stopped.

"They can't stop radio signals and TV signals from coming over that wall." (Today that actually might be possible, but not back then.)

He continued. "You only get the bullshit from the Western media. I get the bullshit from the Western media *and* the Eastern media. I know more about what is really going on than you do."

He had a point—at least I thought he might. Maybe I *was* only getting one perspective. Was I, with my attitude and orientation and perspective, as much a product of wall-to-wall propaganda as Frank's? I wasn't quite prepared to concede the causal relativeness of truth. *Our media bullshit versus their media bullshit?* It couldn't be that simple.

That was my wake up call. My first, "Okay, maybe there is more going on here than I thought," moment. I didn't think I was necessarily wrong about what I knew—or what I thought I knew. What I felt—and it really was more of a physical sensation than mental intuition—was that more was going on than I realized. There was more to it than having one or two of my biases confirmed. I could know more. For instance, at the time I had no clue that anyone behind the Wall had access to Western media at all. Duh? Right? I mean, how hard could it really have been?

I was in such a euphoric state at the time…well, let's just say that I don't think I came across as an Einstein to my communist friends. We started asking them questions. The most obvious curiosity was what it was like living in a communist state. *My Frank* was very frank (no pun intended). I remember exactly what he said.

"Well, you know, I just don't wake up in the morning and think to myself, *Oh, shit*,"—and he kind of made one of those comical slaps to the forehead—*"communist country, what am I going to do today?"* He said, "I wake up. I brush my teeth. Have a shower. Have some breakfast. Pack up my things, and go to school."

However, he did say that one could not trust just anyone. Or at least, one had to be suspicious of anyone and everyone. The Stasi, the secret police of the German Democratic Republic, and the snoops and informants could be anywhere. They could be your father or your neighbour. One did not know who to trust at all, or who could turn on you.

Frank said he was always very careful and had to preface every political discussion with, "You know, comrade, Marxist-Leninist system is the best system in the world, and I would not want to live any other way. But…we could improve it a little bit if we were to do this or to do that."

It was a preamble—it sounded like nonsense—but it was level-headed and obligatory. He said it many times—countless times. "The communist system is the best way to go, but…" It was the opening refrain to every such discussion. It was their ritual.

I asked him about music. He asked me what music I thought he liked. In hindsight, I realize he had probably already pegged me as this green Westerner, sizing me up as a person with limited knowledge of what it truly meant to be living behind the Iron Curtain.

So I said, Bach, Beethoven. Wagner. You know, the heavy hitters of classical music.

He said, "No. Beatles!"

"Beatles? No kidding. You know the Beatles?"

"So what song do you think is my favourite song?"

Of course, my mind was still trapped in that set of cultural expectations.

I was still thinking something classic and in the Beatles sense, ballads. *"Let It Be. Hey, Jude."*

"No, no, no," he said. *"Back in the U-S-S-R."*

We had a good laugh—at me! Again.

We talked about my recent travelling adventures and working on the kibbutz, declaring to them I was Jewish. That elicited no particularly demonstrative reaction from either of the Franks. The two Americans were not Jewish. I did not know it at the time, nor did he tell me then, but years later Frank divulged to me that I had been the first Jew he had ever met.

In Frank's special way, he was determined to not let my statement go without an affable nod that he heard me, and sensed an opportunity for *bridge building*.

There was a small population of Jewish people in East Berlin at the time, Frank said, though not many their age. I wondered how he readily knew the demographics of East Berlin. He was also interested in my experiences on the kibbutz. They continued showing us around, pointing out different sights and we endlessly shared many more stories along the way.

As we strolled around the streets of East Berlin, it was impossible not to notice the East Berlin side of the Wall, which was pristine in sharp contrast to the West Berlin side of the Wall that was covered with political graffiti. It was a constant reminder of the authoritarian state in which they lived. People died attempting to escape that control. But for me, I could leave unobstructed and peacefully.

When it was time to leave, I asked *my Frank* if he would mind giving me his address. I said I would love to stay in touch. Toronto had once seemed so far away and detached from East Berlin. I was hoping to bridge the gap.

He agreed, and we exchanged addresses. The last entry in my diary for June 12, 1983 reads:

>*...A truly remarkable visit, tremendously enlightening and rewarding. I will stay in touch with Frank H [my Frank].*
>
>*...*

In the planning stages for this trip of a lifetime, East Berlin wasn't even a consideration. Had I never taken that detour, however, I don't even want to contemplate that scenario and where I would be today.

CHAPTER 2

DÉTENTE

> Life can only be understood backwards; but it must be lived forwards.
> —Søren Kierkegaard

July 16, 1983
Hello, Frank.
I hope that you are well and that all your examinations were successful. By the time that you receive this letter I will be back in Israel trying to learn Hebrew. This past month I have been here in England visiting with my relatives (I think I told you that I was born here) so except for a wild week in London I've been resting and eating a lot. I've put on at least three kilos.

When I left Berlin I visited Copenhagen and Stockholm for about two weeks. Frank, I have never seen such beautiful girls in my life as there are there. And so many of them!

From there I went to Amsterdam for a couple of days. There are some fantastic museums in

Amsterdam. I really loved the Van Gogh museum. Aside from his works there were also works of other Impressionists like Monet, Cezanne, Renoir, Lautrec and others. Also visited Anne Frank's House. I'm sure that you've heard of her, from WWII; it was very touching to be there.

From Amsterdam I went to England and that has been my tour through Europe, the west and just a touch of the eastern side, right? I think that nothing was more memorable for me than going to Berlin, especially East Berlin and meeting you and Frank. It was probably the most enlightening two hours I've spent in a long time. I certainly have a better understanding, and a less clouded impression of what your life is really like there. I must say that at least for you and Frank things look pretty good.

I can't believe that I'll be back in Israel (my homeland?) so soon. I am looking forward to it, to see some friends at my old kibbutz and just to be back in the country. This should be a major test for me, to see if I would ever live there, if I can learn the language well, and even to see how I can deal with the summer heat which will go as high as 40 degrees to 45 degrees.

If you get a chance to write that would be great, but please, no German (Deutsch?) I would barely understand a word.

I look forward to hearing from you. Say hello to Frank for me. I wish you both the greatest success in your medical studies.

Until then, your friend,
Stuart

My very first letter to Frank was written from my aunt's home in Manchester, England. I couldn't wait to begin the correspondence with my communist friend, but never could have imagined where it would lead.

I note my huge interest in the museums I visited in Europe, even listing the great Impressionist artists who most captivated me; while implying between the lines that I was something of a sophisticate when it comes to art. As one can see from my comical misspelling of Henri de Toulouse-Lautrec, I was about as raw as they come.

Prior to this trip, I had virtually no firsthand experience with art. In fact, my introduction to the joys of Impressionism was the direct result of a romantic tryst in Paris where a beautiful older Vancouverite woman dragged me to the Musée d'Orsay. What choice did I have? Despite my pretensions to the contrary, it was Frank who always impressed for his wide range of interest in literature, art, film, and music.

I went on to tell Frank how "enlightening" that day in Berlin had been for me. I would use the same description when I told anyone about my year-long sojourn through Europe and Israel.

Interestingly, it would be years later that I would realize that I rarely used the word "enlightening" to describe anything else.

I was always fascinated by world events and that was what motivated me to study politics at university. We had ready access to the major US network TV stations, and I devotedly watched those Buffalo stations for news. Then came Vietnam in all its bloody infamy. Had I been older I would have probably been a John Kennedy groupie. In high school I wrote a report on the Cuban Missile Crisis; I had incredible admiration for JFK.

I was a very serious child—especially about politics.

I will never forget waking up bright and early on June 5, 1968. It was so significant to me that my father's thirty-eighth birthday fell on the same date that Robert Kennedy had been shot at the Ambassador Hotel in Los Angeles just a couple of hours earlier. I ran into my parent's bedroom to wake them up to tell them the terrible news. RFK died the following day. One of the memories I have of my father is sitting with him on the couch in our apartment watching the funeral at St. Patrick's Cathedral in New York.

Hilariously, what I did not tell Frank in that first letter was that after Berlin, I went to Paris with an American actor who was an accomplished ladies man, and that we had some wild adventures (including my aforementioned introduction to Impressionist art!). I was thinking that casual sex might not be something that communists neither approved of nor indulged in.

In the context of forever being engrossed in and aware of modern geopolitics, the Warsaw Pact countries and the USSR were an inconceivable abnormality to me. Having had a chance to talk with Frank in East Berlin was something I had never imagined was possible. Its impact on me was indelible and impossible to exaggerate. That is still true, even after all these years. The Cold War—the stark divisions between *us* and *them*—appeared such a clear and permanent condition to me. It seemed unimaginable that the two sides could ever reconcile.

* * * *

My first letter from Frank arrived about a month later. He began by telling me that he was in the middle of a lecture, but felt like writing instead. Students are the same all over!

Frank enjoyed travelling as much as I did. Of course, travel for him was restricted to countries within the Soviet Bloc. Even so, he seemed to have explored more of the world than I had. He wrote to me about his holiday in Russia, Georgia, and Armenia. I assumed part of Frank's appetite for new experiences was simply a normal response to not having much. I wondered how "different" these mostly grey communist countries could be from one another. I was a bit smug about it. Frank would write to me often of his travels and in great and memorable detail. It was always amazing and fascinating to hear about his experiences, and how much joy he seemed to take from those he met along the way. It looked like he had his priorities straight.

His nature is to find the best in everything. I am not sure I could say the same thing about myself—not at the time, anyway.

I shared his wanderlust. My Eurail Pass suited me to a T; it was freedom. But while Frank, too, loved to travel, he also seemed to enjoy being where he was—whereas I was restless and always wanted to be somewhere else. Frank found an extension of himself in travel, while I was looking for distraction through it.

It is said that some people are all about the going and not about the getting there. That was me.

> *...My friend and I slept in a tent and took a bath in a cold stream and made a fire for tea. It felt very good. What a man likes! I thought of Hemingway*

and his view of man and friendship, and I had to smile.

...

The first time I read Hemingway was not long ago. Alas!

> ...*It's best to see a country by yourself. To see how the simple people live and to have contact with them. To speak with them, to have a drink with them and laugh. In school we learn Russian. Of course that is very important. We got a sense for their problems. For their life. And when we sit together with the people and drink, we have a toast for peace and friendship. For they are not so interested in material things and are less hectic. They don't know stress. If there is money they spend and live good. If not, they improvise. For me this huge country with its many nations has a special fascination.*
>
> *Excuse my bad English.*
>
> *Later. It's 11 PM. I'm sitting in my armchair smoking a pipe drinking tea listening to music Supertramp—a new record which I bought two weeks ago in Budapest. That's the situation. Do I need more?*

...

It's a reasonable question. Do we need more? I did. It was a bit ironic to me that my bias about the Soviet Bloc was that they had nothing and the West had everything; but here was Frank, implying his ideal life would be to have *even less*. I, on the other hand, needed more. Or rather, what I thought I needed was something different.

In an effort to find that elusive answer to what I yearned for, I returned to Israel from England—six months into this extended journey. My plan was to learn the language of the land and enrolled in a Hebrew immersion program with the thought of possibly moving there permanently.

My first few months in Israel transformed me into a committed secular Zionist. For the first time in my life, I became fiercely proud of the miracle that was Israel and also to be Jewish. I still vividly remember looking through the window of the airplane and getting a glimpse of that first view of Israel. It was home.

I was not happy in Canada. And moving to Israel in my early twenties meant that I would be drafted in the army. I thought about that, but it was not a hindrance. It just came with the territory. After all, I had been a tough Canadian hockey player. I could take care of myself.

> *October 12, 1983*
> *Dear Frank,*
> *First of all I hope that all is well with you and that you are progressing well at the university.*
> *I got a great surprise these last two days. Yesterday I received two letters from you and today the postcard arrived from Armenia. It seems as though the mail delivery between there and Israel is very slow, it doesn't matter I was just very happy to hear from you. I have left the other kibbutz to come back to the one that I was at originally (the letters and the postcards you sent were forwarded to me here at Kibbutz Massada, not the same place as the Mount Masada that you might have studied about in history class). I didn't enjoy the life on the other kibbutz, though after my two months that I stayed there I did learn a lot of Hebrew; hopefully that will*

prepare me enough in case I decide to live here in Israel within the next two years or so.

It is very interesting to be in Israel at this particular time. We have had the Israeli army pull back the troops in Lebanon, Prime Minister Begin resigning, and the economy is getting worse each day. For example, in the next three months prices will go up at least 50 percent, making the inflation for 1983 at 190 percent. I buy something in the shop today and tomorrow it costs 12 percent more; you have to see it to believe it. You know, Israel has many problems with her Arab neighbours, the West Bank, the Gaza etc., but the greatest problem facing Israel is from within, the internal problems of living in this country.

This country is not worried about losing a war. She is far too strong, every day I see the fighter jets in the skies, soldiers everywhere, this truly is one of the best armies in the world. But there are great problems in the country between the religious Jewish and non-religious, between the Jewish person from the Mediterranean and African areas, and the European Jew, and the economy are serious problems. I'm leaving the country in a few weeks. I will write again before I leave and tell you more about what I've done.

Take care!

Stuart

I was hitchhiking in Israel from Kibbutz Massada to the nearby city of Tiberias and was picked up by a man driving a small truck. His deportment was sour, which matched his disheveled appearance and I wondered why he even stopped to pick up a stranger. I soon learned he spoke English reasonably well and struck up a conversation.

I could barely complete my statement about what a wonderful and exciting country Israel was that he disparagingly began citing all the domestic problems facing her. I responded with a proud statement that formed as a question, "But what about the military?"

He scoffed and grunted at the suggestion. Giving it "the old college try" I retorted, "How about Entebbe?" Almost six years earlier, elite commandos of the Israeli Defence Force launched a daring counter-terrorist rescue at the Entebbe airport in Uganda, freeing the mostly Jewish hostages of an Air France flight from Tel Aviv originally bound for Paris. The truck driver's face glowed, and if he were a peacock his bright and spectacular plumage would have been on full display. "Ah, *then* we were great!" the driver replied.

I was slowly learning more about my heritage and that of Israel, both rather complex.

There is a famous episode in the history of Jerusalem when the Jews rebelled against the Romans in 66 CE. The Jews were heavily outnumbered by Titus's soldiers, but according to the chronicler Josephus they could have held out but for one thing: incessant squabbling amongst factions of the Jews inside Jerusalem. In biblical Hebrew there is a term for this: *Sinat Chinam* (baseless hatred amongst fellow Jews). *Sinat Chinam* destroyed the Second Temple and its eradication will purportedly lead to unity of the Jewish people today. I wasn't thinking of this when I wrote to Frank, but I think it is undeniable that one of the greatest strengths of the Jewish people is our uncompromising solidarity but mostly when threatened by an external enemy.

Over the ages, Jewish people have always felt we have been in the minority and have faced terrible odds against our survival, but have always persevered no matter what tragedy has befallen us. I was beginning to strongly identify with the Jewish sense of collective self-preservation. Us against all of those who would do us harm. *Us vs. Them;* it is a recurring—virtually a permanent—theme of being Jewish.

I am not so sure anymore that the lines can be so easily drawn. Solidarity is a necessary antidote to strife and division, but solidarity is dangerous when it becomes a permanent state of mind.

I left Ma'agan Michael, the kibbutz ulpan (Hebrew immersion) program where I had enrolled. It hadn't worked out as planned, and I decided to move on; I wanted my trip to end on a high note, so I returned to Kibbutz Massada where I had been so happy before. Frank's letters caught up with me there.

It felt great to receive two letters and one postcard in two days from Frank. I said how excited and happy to hear from him I was. It was true. Of all places, I thought, I am receiving correspondence from behind the Iron Curtain! I felt special. Privileged. Extraordinary. Here I was, a Canadian from Toronto working and living on a kibbutz in Israel and I had a friend in a communist country corresponding with me—how cool was that?

But while there was a small détente occurring inside of me regarding my relationship with one German member of a Warsaw Pact country, I was more than aware of the oddity of it, nonetheless. It was uncomfortable.

I had not grown up feeling that I was a victim of anti-Semitism. As a Jew, however, how could I not have lingering feelings of loathing about the Germans in particular? But the war and the Holocaust was not a personal experience for me. The friends I had—at home and on the kibbutz—many were from families of survivors. But my family wasn't. Nonetheless, for some reason Frank struck me from the very beginning as an exception. "I will keep in touch with Frank H." Probably my background in political science was a factor, as was my interest in Cold War politics. And, let's face it, my sense of my own Jewish identity was still a work in progress. I was a Zionist, but my passions were predominantly secular in nature. My curiosity in Frank and his life in Communist East Berlin far outweighed any religious or historical issues.

As the relationship unfolded, even in those early days, a wall was beginning to erect.

There was one thing about Frank that I was dying to know. *Frank,* I wanted to ask, *what did your father do in the war?*

CHAPTER 3

FORMED BY THE PAST

> Your past is always your past. Even if you forget
> it, it remembers you.
> —Sarah Dessen

My father's parents were born in Manchester, England. My father, Roy, was born in 1930, also in Manchester.

My mother, Hazel, was born in Leeds in 1935. She was the middle of three Cohen sisters. My father had one older sibling, Estelle. During the war, because of Nazi bombings I was told the Cohen's moved from Leeds to Manchester.

On my mother's side of the family I am the fourth generation born in the UK. My great grandmother on my father's side supposedly was impregnated by either a count or someone of nobility in Budapest, Hungary. She was forced to leave Budapest, and ended up in the UK. The rest of her family stayed behind and perished in the Holocaust. I only learned about this in recent years. Up until then, I had assumed the Holocaust hadn't touched us—well, me—at all.

My father was not born as a Lewis. He was a Bergman. His mother remarried when he was about twenty to a man named Jack Lewis. In England in the 1950s it was very challenging to be a Jewish businessman. "Lewis" was much less of a "Jewish-sounding" name. So my father had his name legally changed to Lewis. My grandmother Gertie was in the textile business in Wigan, just west of Manchester; she was a tough and independent woman. She made a good living at a time when many women weren't entrepreneurs. Gertie was short and stout who loved singing in amateur opera. I assume it was her rotund figure that gave her the barrel-sized voice I can never forget.

I don't know much about my paternal grandfather. My father told me that he would only see his father once or twice per year. He died of lung cancer at age fifty-five. As a soldier during WWI he was gassed in battle. Dad also said to me that he didn't much like his father.

My maternal grandfather was a tailor. That was a common Jewish vocation at the time, and one of the few where the Jews were readily accepted by the non-Jewish. He worked for one company most of his life. My grandmother Doris never worked outside the home. She was a tough lady, too, with a very hard exterior. My Grandpa Mark was a soft, sweet, and lovely man—angelic. They were quite a complement to one another.

In 1959 my family immigrated to Canada when I was still an infant.

My father was a travelling salesman and was often away from home. On very rare occasions my mother has alluded to the fact that us being in Canada may have been due to him having to escape England, but it was not discussed, primarily because I did not want to know. When he left a steady job he had in the early 1970s and went into the import/export business on his own, the story turns more murky. I was never fully aware of my father's business dealings.

The few times we vacationed it was predominantly to England. The first time we returned, I was two years old and I was with my mother alone; I assume my father was away on business, but maybe that was not the case. In fact, the only time all four of us went together on a family trip to the UK was when I was seven. My brother was two. A pivotal and life-altering moment for me was at ten years of age when, unaccompanied by a parent, I flew alone to England. It was scary, but exhilarating. In some ways when I was growing up I felt the need to be closer to my UK family than my own. They appeared stable and "normal". They all lived in homes, drove nice cars, and appeared to lead full lives. My extended family in England was traditionally (non-religious) Jewish, resembling what I had seen with many of my friends' families in Toronto.

I journeyed to England several more times on my own as a young teenager. I often joined my UK family on their domestic vacations and those were wonderful times. When I returned at age sixteen I became restless and craved more adventure beyond the confines of the UK. So I announced I was heading to Paris for a weekend on my own! It was worth it, despite the concern on both sides of the Atlantic.

All in all, it always felt comforting to be with my UK family. They remain an important element of my life.

The experiences many of my English cousins had of anti-Semitism were foreign to me. They told me about their run-ins with the *"yobs"* (aggressive, violent or rowdy young men) and being roughed up by them on the way home from school.

My father was always a mystery to me. Something was askew in our relationship as I compared it to others.

In many ways, he had a rather stereotypical British demeanor. He would call me "Old Boy" and had the charm of James Bond (a nickname bestowed on him by a couple of childhood friends)—but with me, he always seemed remote and hard to reach below the surface. He gave the impression of a very tough man. I have some good memories of the time he was home and not travelling. He took me to my first NHL hockey game between the Leafs and the Rangers as we sat right behind the Rangers bench. He liked to watch hockey on TV with me, directing my attention to the rough-house style of play, encouraging me to do the same in my games. I was a very aggressive hockey player. I loved throwing my weight around (what weight I had). I hit a lot, which is not allowed in today's game at that age level. I rightfully earned a lot of penalties, mostly for boarding, elbowing and charging. Years later before he left us, my father reminded me how tough I was even as a young player. This is how he wanted me to play, and I took great pride in it and pleasing him.

He worked for a company that was in the commercial upholstery business and he travelled all over the world for them. He talked in a braggadocious manner about his job, but we never had much money so I am not sure how successful he actually was. He travelled a lot to Asia and that sounded very exotic and important to me.

He told stories of his scraps in his youth—about having been beaten up by the *"yobs"* of Manchester just as my cousins had many years later—and one incident in particular. Three boys jumped him and did a number on him. For revenge, he went after the three but separately, one at a time. Like so much of what my father told me, I was never sure what I could believe.

My father was very fit. Not so in a muscular sense, but he was tall, broad and confident of his strength. My brother and I were in the car with Dad one day and where we were headed I don't recall. I must have been about twelve. Suddenly, Dad started shouting out the window and hit the brakes while simultaneously shoving the gearshift into park. It is a miracle he didn't obliterate the transmission. We were in the middle of traffic, but he jumped out and stormed up to the car in front of us and leaned into the open window as if he was going to strangle the driver.

It was a young couple in their twenties at most, and I saw the driver jumping sideways toward his female passenger and putting his hands up defensively while the whole time this "crazy old man" was screaming at them.

They eventually drove off and my father walked back to our car, got in and drove off. We didn't say a word. He didn't, either. We just drove the rest of the way in complete silence.

We lived in an apartment with an outdoor pool and this was where I taught myself how to swim—and I was a pretty good teacher! When my father would return from a business trip, I would demonstrate my progress by swimming lengths and he would pay me for each one. That's how I learned. It seemed okay at the time, but it was a bit like a trained seal in a circus.

I wasn't always aware of it, but money was an issue; although we didn't seem poor at all in my experience. At home he appeared to be a good father. I thought so, anyway. Whatever it was, it was my normal.

Very shortly after my parents separated, he came home to the apartment and announced that he was going away on yet another business trip. It was January 1974. I was fourteen. I thought nothing of it. I remember him specifically saying he would be back for my brother's birthday. He didn't make it.

Several months later, on a day when Dad said he was scheduled to arrive back, Harvey, a family friend, took me to the airport to pick him up. We waited. And waited. He never showed. We drove home in silence. My mother tried to make the best of it. Needless to say, it was an exceptionally painful experience. This happened one more time. We showed up at the airport expecting to greet my father, but he never appeared.

In those days there wasn't much divorce, so this was a big deal. Up until that time, my mother had been a very typical and proud homemaker. And suddenly, she was left on her own with no means of support.

My mother worked up to three jobs a day, seven days a week. My brother and I became very much by necessity—latchkey kids. But our mother kept us out of subsidized housing, which would have been a lot cheaper for her, but meant moving to a less than desirable neighbourhood.

Mom was devotedly and lovingly taking care of us and fought daily to keep a roof over our heads and food in our bellies. When faced with the massive obstacles confronting her, what was more important than that? My father had relinquished that responsibility. Prior to Dad leaving, Mom had never worked in Canada. She never went to college and at the time held no discernible workplace skills. But she did what she had to do. I love and respect her so much for that. Her intestinal fortitude was unparalleled, and I will put her example up to anyone. I don't believe anyone will ever come close to what she was able to accomplish.

She undoubtedly did an amazing job raising my brother and I. I got along well with her, but I don't have many memories of doing things with her except teaching me how to drive—a momentous experience for a young man. And I fondly remember how she washed my hair in the sink after consecutive sport injuries—a broken leg and only months later, a broken arm. She has memories of me being her rock. Me? A fourteen year-old son? I suppose those younger than I have had to step up, as well. After my father left without providing any support, she worked so hard that she was rarely home much, either, and until she met Gil (she would later remarry to him), "fun" had not been a part of her life for a long time.

I had been a very good student—always As and Bs—until the year my father left. This happened during my grade eighth year and that is when my marks started coming down. I really should have failed grade nine. Teachers who knew what was going on at home passed me on to high school. My grades rebounded to average later on, but I had to go to summer school to relearn a couple of courses.

At the time I wasn't aware of it happening. Some kids just stumble at one point, or hit a wall. I never really had to study much up until that point. But I absolutely fell off a cliff with my marks. I wasn't in a bad crowd. I had the same great friends; I continued to play hockey. I really couldn't explain it. Now I don't think there are any coincidences.

I did not enjoy high school and was frequently unhappy, overly serious and often depressed, at least when I wasn't playing sports. I had friends in the in-crowd but I was not in the in-crowd. Sports carried me. I was tall (reached my adult height by fifteen), thin, but quite athletic. I was usually one of the first selected in team pick-up sports at school. I was also the straight arrow. I never drank. A few friends will remember having plans with me, but I would never show up—later claiming that I had suddenly fallen asleep, which I did, but it was by no accident. Sometimes I thought it was better to be alone. I had a small circle of friends—mostly Jewish and some of whom I am still friends with today. My high school was eighty-five percent Jewish and the rest were Italian; there were one or two African Canadian students. A good number of the kids came from well-to-do families—or so it appeared to me from my vantage point—and I didn't like it. I suppose I had a huge chip on my shoulder about my father, as well. I felt cheated.

My father always taught me (or shall I say *wanted* me to be) tough—and disapproved of what he perceived as weakness.

I was liked in school, but I think I was boring. I would meet girls, yet their mothers liked me more than their daughters did! I had a perennial summer job as a carnie at The Ex (the CNE—Canadian National Exhibition) in Toronto, and this job aided me in coming out of my introverted shell. I was, without doubt, the world's worst carnie. I was shy and my job required that I verbally lure people into playing ball toss games (like Tic-Tac-Toe and Bushel Baskets). Oh, I was horrible. I think most people who bought in probably felt sorry for me and at the same time could take advantage of me—many did. Looking back on it, it is astonishing to me that so much of what I did for jobs in my life was sales, even at such a young age—the very thing I promised myself later that I would never do. It was like my father, even when he was absent from my life, still had this incredible influence on me.

I can't say by growing up in Toronto that I really felt anti-Semitism directly. It wasn't until my freshman week at Carleton University that I experienced anti-Semitism firsthand. One evening I was hanging out in the TV room of our co-ed residence, and a student started telling this joke about "putting Jews in the ovens" and the Holocaust. There might have been six or seven others sitting around. A fuse in me lit; outwardly I was calm, but inside I thought I was going to explode. I stood up and walked over to the freshman offender and put my hand on his chest and very coolly but forcefully thrust him hard up against a wall.

Face-to-face—literally—I said, "I don't ever want to hear that type of joke again." That was it.

He had to know that I had been pushed to a point where he would be fearful of it happening again. Mostly, I think he was shocked. And he seemed confused, with an accusatory face that said, "What is a *real* Jew doing here?" We lived on the same floor, yet he never said another word to me. Not one.

I know I was the first Jew a lot of kids had ever met once I left the cocoon of high school. An abundant number of Carleton students came from smaller towns and cities all across Canada and many international students attended there, as well. I recall another time I was chatting with a friend from Calgary. I can't remember how it came up, but I told her I was Jewish.

She said, "You aren't Jewish." I said, "Yeah." She looked at me like a mother would a recalcitrant child. "Stuart, you're not Jewish." She just would not believe that I was actually Jewish. And of course, that started me thinking. *What did she think a Jewish person looked like?*

So I said again. "Listen, I am. I *am* Jewish. Okay?" It went back-and-forth. Honestly, it was surreal and the longer it went on, the more ridiculous it became. *So this is a friendly argument just about the status of my religion by birth? Seriously?* I am not sure whether she actually believed me or simply lost interest, but she finally replied, "Okay, you're Jewish." We got past that; we were good friends, but it was so weird. I even had some fellow floormates resent the fact that I, a Jew, was Santa Claus during our floor Christmas party. I also resented it after I caught mononucleosis from one of the gifts *I* received!

The Jewish kids in high school had been mostly secular. I learned later, however, that far more were religiously observant than I had thought. They hid their identity on purpose for fear of appearing weird and becoming unpopular. Looking back, I think it was the subtle incidents like these—hiding one's identity; having to defend one's identity—that set me on my own complicated path of self-discovery.

It wasn't really until university that I realized I had an identity that needed defending. At Carleton, of course, I didn't know a soul and in those days the criteria for matching kids up with compatible roommates was based on smoking habits. My roommate and I were non-smokers.

My first year roommate was a pretty laid back sort of guy who was a very experienced drinker, especially with beer. I became very impressed when he said his real passion was for a mixed drink called a Black Russian. When he described the contents of that drink, I realized it was too much alcohol for me! He and I got along famously well. His family even took me on a couple of skiing trips with them into the Laurentian Mountains, and for many years I was a welcomed guest on Boxing Day to their Southwestern Ontario home.

One day on campus, there was some activity around Holocaust remembrance, and when we met up later he made the following comment to me: "Can't you guys just stop with the Holocaust and let it go? You always bring it up. That was a long time ago, Stu."

I can see the look on his face now. It was entirely absent of malice; it was like he was comparing the experience of the Jews in the Holocaust with being short-changed at a Tim Horton's. *Why can't we get over it?*

I know people who can't get over the loss of a Stanley Cup playoff series twenty years ago—but here was this otherwise lovely guy telling me that it was time for me to get over the murder of six million Jews!

Years later, something similar happened at work. I was just beginning to deeply appreciate and observe the Jewish holidays. It was Passover, and I had brought matzah (the religiously mandated unleavened bread) to work with me, as was common for many Jews, observant or otherwise. I had a colleague who was the Don Rickles of religiously based one-liners; he never missed an opportunity for mockery. My colleague saw me break out my matzah at lunch.

"Stuart!" he called out. "Is Passover the holiday when Jews kill Christian babies and drink their blood?"

Much to my shock at the statement and embarrassment, at the time I had not yet learned about the blood libel myths from the Middle Ages accusing the Jews of murdering Christian children and using their blood in the preparation of matzah. I laughed and said, "Let me check and I will let you know." Coincidentally, at the time I was reading Chaim Potok's

Wanderings, the history of the Jews and a few days later came across descriptions of the notorious blood libel.

I thought about the joke and found myself growing very angry. Suddenly, the spilling of some Christian blood—Terry's in particular—didn't seem like such a bad idea. But I was mostly confused.

Why would anyone think it was okay to make that kind of joke? The next time I saw him, I decided to ask.

"Why did you make that joke about Jews killing Christian babies?"

He looked innocently at me. "I don't know," he shrugged. I asked him again—calmly—and again he answered, "I don't *know*." I asked again and again. Finally, he blurted—in an exasperated tone—"I don't know. I just did, okay? *What's the big deal?"*

Jesus, Stuart, it's just a joke. Relax, man.

We are all products of a cultural mindset. One doesn't need to be a historian of genocide, however, to know that even the most abominable accusations or libels—if repeated often enough—will be accepted eventually as truth. We see the racist; we don't see racialism. And what I mean by racialism is simply the complex set of social behaviours we accept as normal and reinforced by repetition. And of course, those norms change over time.

It is highly offensive these days to make a joke about an LGBTQ person. It is less offensive, however, to make a joke about the intelligence of blondes. It is perfectly appropriate to make insulting jokes about lawyers or politicians. What does it mean to be offensive?

It all depends on who is offended.

What's the big deal? Why can't you just get over it?

There is a point when the "I" becomes "us" and the "we" becomes "them". That point was coming for me; I was moving towards it, or I was already there.

My past was dictating my future—it seemed inevitable.

CHAPTER 4

HOME BUT NOT *HOME*

> To confront a person in his own shadow is to show him his own light.
> —Carl Jung

January 15, 1984
Dear Frank,
Please forgive me for not having written back sooner. I have been home now for two months and it has taken me awhile to settle down and begin writing to people that I met over the eleven months of my travels. I did send you a picture postcard from Israel before I left, which I hope you received. I enjoyed my return to Israel and now I can speak some Hebrew, though of course I have a long way to go before I will become fluent. How is your English coming along?

I enjoyed reading your letters that I received in Israel, though it did take months for them to reach me. I suppose that there is not a lot of mail that is sent between Israel and the DDR, but I expect that the service is better between Canada and your country. I feel much different being in Canada now than before I left. I can judge this country in a different way now that I've seen places so totally alien to this way of life, and I don't like what I see here now, though I don't consider myself a socialist. Maybe I could be called, as they say, a "bleeding-heart liberal" (I can't translate that, maybe you understand?)...

I was feeling more lost than ever. I had absolutely no direction—unless a circle is a direction. To be honest, I envied Frank being in medical school. Oftentimes I flirted with the idea of enrolling in law school. In the back of my mind I also had this fantasy that one day I might enter politics. I'd like to think I was serious about it, but honestly, I am not sure.

Travelling had been ideal for me. Having no fixed address and no destination had temporarily solved my problems. I loved being on the move. Back in Toronto I was a fish out of water again. I had absolutely no real idea what I wanted to do, and what I was doing I mostly hated.

Being a success really is important to most Jewish people. Rising to the top is not just about the money; it's a pride thing. It's showing everyone that we're still here. *You tried to wipe us out, but we're here.* And we strive to be the best. I, however, at the age of *twenty-four* felt I was floundering; I was getting down on myself. It was hard being surrounded by successful people everywhere I looked and then there was me, without any direction.

...I think that you might enjoy this story. We have here what are called lotteries, which is legalized gambling. Millions of Canadians give one dollar and hope to win a million dollars. Well, one such lottery hadn't had a winner for several weeks so the first

prize was continually getting larger until the prize was 6 million dollars. I didn't win.

This lottery business is not unique to Canada; I think that all the Western countries have them. You can see how money is so important to everyone here, it is terrible but I, like most others, seem to be searching for ways to get it and not just enough to live as they say "comfortably" but to have so much that you don't know what to do with it. But just this morning on the news I hear that people are actually hungry in North America. You should see our grocery stores, shelves always full with food yet people are hungry, of course, not a lot, but they exist. Hard to believe. That's all for now. Good luck in your studies.

Your friend,
Stuart

What is a "bleeding-heart liberal"? Was that me? The dichotomy of what I was exposed to in Israel (especially on the commune-based kibbutz society) and socialist East Berlin versus the juxtaposition of full shelves of food back in Canada, and the nonsense of chasing lottery wins shook me up a bit.

In 1982 I was twenty-two and all I dreamed about was travelling—the farther, the better. I thought about Australia. It sounded about as remote and distant as anyone could go. And that seemed perfect to me.

At the time I was selling home insulation door to door. My friend had an office supply company so I was also driving a truck and delivering office supplies. I also sold suits at a posh menswear store in suburban Toronto. All dead-end jobs as far as I was concerned, not leading me to anything I would consider a long-term career. I stopped caring about the job. My goal was to build up a store of funds so I could travel and busting my ass in these disparate jobs enabled me to realize that goal.

All I could think about was escape.

That June, my aunties Maureen and Judith came to Toronto for a visit. I hadn't booked my trip yet, but it was only a matter of time. My aunts wondered why I picked Australia. *Why not Israel?* they prodded me.

Why would I want to go to Israel? It wasn't an option I had considered at all. I wanted to try something new. But the thought percolated in my head as a great potential for adventure. Then, a friend of mine with whom I had briefly lost touch with told me about a recent trip he made to Israel where he worked on a kibbutz banana plantation. Within two weeks I completely shifted gears. It wasn't because I was a Zionist or a proud Jew. I wasn't; I'm not sure I even knew what that meant at that point. Working on a banana plantation just sounded so exciting.

On December 29, 1982, I boarded an evening flight to Israel and landed in Tel Aviv the following day. It's like it was yesterday. As we were landing—I remember catching a glimpse of the land off the Mediterranean coast and those glorious beaches and the unmistakable Tel Aviv skyline. I got goose bumps. I felt like I was home.

I never expected such an extreme reaction, but I honestly did feel that I was home. It sounds crazy feeling one is home in a place they have never been, not even having set foot upon the land or smelled the air. But before the plane even touched down—from that moment I became a Zionist.

People debate what it means to be a Zionist. But belief in a Jewish homeland; pride in what it took to get there and what it takes to stay…it was etched into me that day, and it stayed with me ever since.

It was so profound. Immediate and unexplainable.

I spent the night in Tel Aviv and made preparations for the bus ride to the kibbutz where I would spend the next four months. Kibbutz Massada is situated just south of the Sea of Galilee, about fifteen minutes down the road from Tiberias, on the border with Jordan and at the foot of the Golan Heights— Israeli-annexed Syrian territory. I also knew that they picked bananas there.

I literally walked into a New Year's Eve party upon my arrival.

What an entrance!

Most of the volunteers on a non-religious kibbutz are non-Jewish, so New Year's Eve was just as one would expect it to be for a few dozen twentysomethings. There were maybe forty volunteers at any given time at Massada, and six at most were Jewish.

Unlike a few years earlier when I shielded my Jewish identity at university, here on the kibbutz I proudly proclaimed it and let it be known within the kibbutz officialdom. I also expressed my preference for working in the banana fields. When I first reported for work, I looked at the posted volunteer worksheet and found my name. And after my name, the word: "security".

Holy shit, I thought. *Security! Just because I am one of the few Jewish volunteers? This is serious!* It was 1983, and tensions between the Jewish people and the Arabs were running high and the kibbutz was right on the Jordanian border. There was a raging war in Lebanon. So...*security? Wow,* I thought. *What the hell have I gotten myself into? What are they going to get me to do? What training in security or self-defence do they think I have?* Maybe I should not have been so quick to tell them I was Jewish.

It turned out the primary responsibility of a volunteer's security job was painting bomb shelter doors. No rifles or camouflage combat gear, just paintbrushes and buckets and buckets of God-awful blue paint. And mostly these bomb shelters were used for storage, and one had been turned into a disco—which was where the previous night's New Year's Eve party took place.

After a few days all the doors had been painted, and I shifted to the banana fields.

I was on Kibbutz Massada for four months and loved everything about the experience. I gained acceptance from others. The physical labour suited me well. In time, I was given supervisory responsibilities in the banana fields. I even played soccer with the Israelis. It was feeling right.

And I fell in love with a beautiful girl who had a boyfriend fighting in the Lebanon War at the time. But I was ready to make a life in Israel with her if given the opportunity. Though we had a purely platonic relationship, others didn't think so. A kibbutz was terribly fertile ground for gossip, like a little village where everyone knows everyone else's business...or so they think! She and I spent a lot of innocent time together, but in that fishbowl environment we would be seen walking around together and it wasn't long before tongues started wagging. She was seventeen and about to go into the army. In addition to her beauty she had a lovely sweet voice and performed often on the kibbutz.

Well, one day she invited me into her apartment to talk—we talked often, but mostly in public. Nothing happened in her apartment. Nothing was going to happen. But word got out. It got ugly. The story that circulated was: while her boyfriend was fighting in Lebanon and risking his life, I was in the blissful safety of the kibbutz apparently "sleeping with his girlfriend." I assumed I was a marked man. Thankfully, nothing of the sort happened. She stayed with him. Bizarrely, *they* now live happily in Canada.

At the end of those four amazing months at Massada, I went to Europe as planned. I was sure I wanted to move to Israel—I just didn't know how or when, with or without the lovely kibbutz girl who stole my heart.

When I came back to Canada from Israel, my Jewish pride was very active and present inside of me. I was convinced I would soon return and even opened a US Dollar bank account to save enough for a one-way ticket to Israel. I also decided to stop dating non-Jewish women. Most, but not all Jewish denominations declare you are Jewish through birth from the mother, not the father. And while I was an unaffiliated Jew, I sided with the more commonly held interpretation. I wanted to have a Jewish family. For the first time in my life, this became important to me. I didn't think of it as racist. It was what I wanted for my future.

> *August 13, 1984*
> Dear Frank,
> Hello my friend! I hope that all is well with you and your family. I wished to write to you sooner, but I've been both lazy (in my letter writing) and also

busy with my endeavours. Did you get the postcards I sent a few months back?

Anyhow, I am at the University of Toronto library. I am studying for my final exam of my final course to complete my B.A. The exam is in six hours, but I just had the urge to write you a quick letter. The course is the history of economic thought of Adam Smith, David Ricardo, and your friend Karl Marx. I think you know "a little" of him! I would have preferred to study the politics of Marx, not just his economics, so in class we're subjected [more] to mathematical expressions than to political philosophies, but on my own time I would like to read some of the works of Marx that you suggested in your last letter.

I am working with my stepfather in business, we manufacture a few products, import some others and my job is basically to sell these things in our retail markets. It is difficult to start a small retail business these days. I still hope to return to Israel next year, I can't seem to get the country out of my blood. It feels like Israel is a part of me and that I belong there, of which I cannot say the same thing about Canada, or the country of my birth, England. I still feel that Canada is the greatest country in the world. I hope that one day you will get the opportunity to visit here, although I don't know if I will still be here. I'll try to meet you though!

Well, Frank, I should get back to my studying. I am quite nervous actually. I'm not sure if I know enough.

I look forward to your letters, as always.
Take care,
Stuart

In that letter it appears as though I was still on the *socialist* track. This was not a serious commitment but a kind of harmless flirtation. What did I know of socialism?

I told Frank that I wanted to read more of Marx. I never did, and what is interesting is that what I was actually attempting was to earn enough money so that I could move to Israel. I was at the University of Toronto finishing up the Bachelor of Arts degree I began at Carleton. It was important for me to finish it, and in 1984 I did.

I wrote that I hoped to return to Israel in 1985. I was ready. I was very unsettled upon my return to Canada, and before I landed my job at Xerox in February 1985, I couldn't stand being there. Israel was home. I was happy there; happy on the kibbutz, happy with its communal lifestyle — I really thought that was what I wanted and needed.

I didn't feel at home in Canada, nor did England feel like a country to put down permanent roots. Israel did. I yearned for that feeling of belonging. A Jewish homeland was just that to me: belonging. I wanted it badly.

> *October 17, 1984*
> *Dear Frank,*
> *Tremendous as always to hear from you. You sound well and it is refreshing to see how much you appear to be enjoying your studies. Thanks for the photograph, it brought back some good memories, especially of that old camera you had; it really does work!*
>
> *I successfully finished that course, part of which included Marx's economics, although my strength in the course was more on Adam Smith than on Karl Marx. It was my final course requirement from the*

BA degree. Now I expect that I will try to get work in the private industry, perhaps in administration. [It may be worth noting that I had no idea at all what I meant by this, nor any clue about what I would do.] *For the time being I am working in a men's clothing store as a salesman, which I detest. It is not very easy to find good employment right now so I can't walk away from my present job until I get more what I am looking for.* [...]

We have had a lot more excitement in Canada recently. First the Pope came to Canada, the first to visit Canada ever. You know that I am not a Catholic, but nonetheless, I found his visit, his words and actions often moved me to emotion. Not in a spiritual nature, but he does leave one with a good feeling, especially when his message and words are non-denominational, of course, he speaks such magnificent words of peace.

...

I was trying to deal with my natural sense of spirituality!

...The Queen was here, too. If you remember, I was born in England, and for the longest time I was very much in favour of the monarchy. I am not anymore. I don't believe that by an accident of birth one should be entitled to such that they receive. The Royal Family are the wealthiest recipients the world has ever seen. Now, I do realize that they lead a rather hectic lifestyle, one which I wouldn't care to have, and the monarchy and the spectacle of Buckingham Palace are worth millions of dollars to British tourism. Still, I strongly believe that the concept of monarchy is archaic and that it has

no place in a world approaching the twenty-first century.

Your vacation to Bulgaria sounds fascinating. Someday I would like to see all the countries that you have visited. […] Tell me, now that you have been to all these countries do you detect many similarities, in culture, in values of the people, in their desires? After travelling through Western Europe, I did notice such similarities. Yes, the scenery was different and language was different, but overall the people were not. They had the same fears and joys, the same goals and aspirations. I wonder if living under the same type of political and economic system has left those under the respective "umbrella" if you will, rather the same.

It is for this reason that I would likely prefer to visit some place very different from Western civilization. […] I think that those cultures would be very exciting to experience. The East–West business is so crazy, isn't it? It seems to have reached all corners of the world. I have been studying the Third World countries recently on my own. Every country has the left fighting the right, all of them are committing such human atrocities it is unthinkable.

I don't blame the Third World countries so much as I blame the USSR and the USA (and not necessarily in that order). If these backward nations want to have civil wars let us sell them clubs or they can just throw rocks at one another. After two hundred years or so they will likely develop their own atomic weapons, but hopefully by then we will have resolved our present state of things and show them the "better way".

> *Anyway, once more, my friend, I have failed to solve the world's problems. I have enjoyed trying though! By the way, Frank, I would like to hear about your family sometime.*
>
> *Continued success in your endeavours.*
> *Your friend,*
> *Stuart*

I casually asked Frank to tell me a bit about his family. It was the first time I broached the issue—albeit indirectly—of family history. I wanted to know what Frank's father did in the war.

This had become a weighty barrier for me—a very high wall. I wanted to know, but I was not sure if I was actually ready. And I didn't know why. I had no worries that whatever Frank said would jeopardize our friendship. Then what?

I expressed my admiration for the Pope—or at least for his message. I have always had a spiritual side (I expect many of us do) and for me, that means a sense of belonging. To believe in something is, after all, to belong to that thing. But what to believe? I wanted to choose a belief system. Frank was inadvertently causing me to think, but I was not ready to understand. I had gravitated to a Jewish way of life, but I can see now that I was ripe to move towards something else if it was presented.

I was moved by the Pope's words of hope and peace. They seemed so logical and straightforward—and universal. I was more than aware of the irony: me, a young Jewish man, being so moved by the inspiring words of the world's most powerful Catholic. The Jews, understandably, have historically had an awkward relationship with the Catholic Church and individual Catholics.

But I think it was about this time when I first had a sense that no one or no denomination had a monopoly on truth—yet it was such a truth that was subconsciously luring me.

It is interesting to me now that I come across as consumed with East–West divisions and the glaring dichotomies between rich and poor. I am disturbed by the entitlement of a monarchy juxtaposed with the concept of a normal day of real work and earning your lot in life. (Probably Frank—the psychoanalyst—would have said I was sublimating!) I was deeply unhappy and frustrated, and I was escaping my unsatisfactory existence into the complicated abstractions and distractions of world politics in my correspondence with him.

I was a liberal growing up: I even dabbled with the Socialist International in university, but I recall worrying about how it could hinder a potential political career later on and abruptly backed out of any further involvement. Kind of like the time when I was parachuting (only one jump), and while slowly coming down to Earth, I attempted to fix the chute's support straps pinching me around my crotch until I also abruptly realized that that, too, was stupid and quite possibly fatal!

Jewish life was beginning to take centre stage. I was not a passionate or religiously committed Jew at that point; however, I felt I had received my awakening. No Jewish person is ever much removed from the Holocaust, and as secular, open-minded, and liberal as I may have imagined myself, I realized I still deeply mistrusted the German people. So why did I open up so readily and easily to Frank? I was burning with questions. I surmised that it was not at all unlikely that Frank's father (or relatives) were soldiers in the war against the Allies. Could they also have been hardcore Nazis?

Was I being dishonest to my people and what would they think?

What did your father do in the war, Frank?

…And yet, all I knew in my heart was that Frank was *not* the enemy. No matter what his father may or may not have been. But I was absolutely curious to know the truth. The past was the elephant in the room.

CHAPTER 5

RITUALS

> Man's search for meaning may arouse inner
> tension rather than inner equilibrium.
> —Viktor Frankl

January 28, 1985
Dear Frank,
I apologize for the delay in not writing sooner. I am rather lazy when it comes to letter writing; I probably mentioned that to you already!
I am sorry to read that you and your girlfriend broke up. I must say that you take a very pragmatic attitude towards the circumstances of the demise of the relationship. I believe that is half the battle to the realization that the relationship is over. The other half has to do with your heart or your soul, and judging by my past experiences we have no control over our hearts. We feel what we feel.
It was interesting to read your comment of President Reagan, that a bad actor is again president of such a nation. But you know, that is really what

this so-called American Dream is all about. Where else but in the USA can it happen? Last week there was a grand party in Washington, DC, for Reagan. It was on TV, of course, and an old movie star named Jimmy Stewart said a few words to the president. He said, "Mr. President, is it true that only in America can a man star in a movie with a monkey one day, and on another day be president of the USA? Just be thankful it doesn't happen the other way around."

I thought that was quite funny.

Well, of course, a lot of talk in the news here today or recently has been about the Star Wars defence plans and new talks in Geneva; oh, and replacement for Chernenko, possibly Gorbachev. I have to agree with you that it is insane to build such weapons, but isn't it also insane that we need talks to tell each other that neither side really wants to blow up the world?!

Here, in Canada, a couple of other issues are receiving heated attention: abortion and capital punishment. It is strange to listen to some right-wing people who are all in favour of the death penalty for murder, but are against abortion because it takes a life. Then there are people on the left who are against the death penalty but favour the choice of a woman to decide the fate of her own body. Of course, the issue is not so black and white.

An old report surfaced this week that Joseph Mengele, nicknamed the Angel of Death, the Nazi doctor of Auschwitz who performed thousands of brutal experiments attempted to emigrate to Canada from Paraguay in 1962. He is likely still in Paraguay, but he may be here. I hope that before Mengele dies of natural causes we get him first. Is that wrong for me to feel this way, even though I told you of my feeling about capital punishment?

I am becoming more and more enthusiastic about moving to Israel. Sounds crazy, doesn't it, especially when one considers all the problems that exist there. Every week or so I attend meetings for people wishing to live there. I'll keep you posted on the path of life I choose.

…

That letter was posted about six months before I met my future wife. My life was about to take a decisive turn.

I had just accepted an excellent sales position from Xerox and the dream of *aliyah*—moving to Israel—was sidelined. Only temporarily, I thought at the time.

At one point I recall saying to myself that I didn't want to go to Israel simply to escape a situation that made me unhappy back home. I was restless, and I think the appeal of putting down roots in Israel was enormously appealing. But I wanted to make sure that when I made *aliyah* I was making a change from a position of strength, not weakness.

"Home" has always been a loaded word for me, and I don't just mean the England-Canada-Israel *home* issue. We lived exclusively in apartments when I was growing up. After my father left and we had no money, we faced eviction and the probability of having to move to government subsidized housing. My mother would have none of it. As I mentioned earlier, she would end up working multiple jobs to make the rent and to keep our disrupted lives appearing as normal as possible. Yet, despite Gil arriving on the scene, Mom was still fiercely independent—working so much of the time. I am not sure I really ever knew what a "normal" home life was.

Some of my happiest non-sports memories of life with my father before he left were our frequent trips to the parking lot roof at the Toronto airport. We'd watch the planes take off and land. I loved it. I was dreaming that I was flying away somewhere. Anywhere.

Maybe my Israel goal was an idealized substitute for the "belonging" home I had always envied other kids having (or my idea of it). I felt I didn't "belong" in my life in Canada; at the time I believed it to be on a kibbutz in Israel. So I searched for that feeling. It was a very tempting and enticing dream. At the same time, I wondered if I was avoiding my reality by dreaming of running away.

In my letters with Frank, I had to insert something new—not quite dishonesty, but omission due to a glaring awareness of our potentially awkward friendship and a most uncomfortable label; in technical terms, as a citizen of a Warsaw Pact country he was "the enemy" and me, a citizen of a NATO member state.

> *March 16, 1985*
> *Dear Frank,*
> *I hope this letter finds you well. I have received good examination results. I have enclosed a photograph for you, I hope that you receive this one, I think it is a good photograph for the little camera that I have.*
> *I really enjoyed your last two letters. I also get excited when I check the mail to see from which part of the world I will receive mail. I did receive your*

letter of 28.1.85 before I received the letter of 12.1.85. I suppose someone was sleeping at the post office.

Frank, your English is superb! I just want to bring something to your attention. You wrote that you enjoyed "drinking a bear" with your friends. Perhaps you see your mistake already? If not, go to your dictionary. I think you will find it amusing! Still, your English is wonderful. I even think it is better than mine sometimes!

Well, we have a new Soviet leader Mikhail Gorbachev. The looks of him, his age and energy, he should be around for quite a long time. I hope this is positive.

I have finally started a new job and it is a good one. I'm working for a multinational company [Xerox] *as a sales representative of photocopiers and other business equipment. Tomorrow the company is sending me to Virginia, USA, for two weeks of sales training. The training centre is only one half-hour from Washington, DC. I'll send you a postcard. Would you like one of the White House or of something important?*

…

My clumsy evasion with Frank about where I was working was not accidental. My contract with Xerox very specifically forbade any transactions or communications with Warsaw Pact countries, and I absolutely did not want anyone in the company knowing about Frank or our correspondence. It was probably an unnecessarily paranoid precaution on my part, but in 1985 I was very aware of it.

It reminds me of how much of daily life back then involved some heavy form of "us" and "them".

Frank was one of my most cherished friends, but my situation with the company had him branded (fairly or not) as *the enemy*. In all those years since, not much has really changed in society. We keep creating enemies, internal and external ones. A president has even been known to label groups of his own people as enemies.

In early April I received a letter from Frank. He was home after exams and was taking it easy listening to the newest Joe Cocker album. He told me that he and his brother had just seen a really wonderful film version of Dostoevsky's *The Brothers Karamazov* and he wondered if I had seen it.

I had not.

Honestly, there were times when I wondered if maybe Frank had adopted me as some kind of bizarre communist-inspired, Aid-to-a-Culturally-Deprived-Westerner campaign. What could it have been that drew him to me? I was always so inspired by Frank, but had a hard time imagining what it was that he was getting from me. He was also reading the newest Kurt Vonnegut novel. In time, I would learn from Frank that life in East Berlin was never as great as he implied, but I was both amazed and surprised how full and rich his life seemed. Books, music, art, museums. What exactly was the Wall keeping out?

> **April 8, 1985**
> Dear Stuart,
> Hello, my dear friend! There is nobody other in the world as you think so often to me.
> Yesterday your first card from Washington DC today your second card for real surprise. Oh boy, you are right! What an imagination, you in the White

House! I think that we would have some trouble fewer in the world. But it is no more but a dream. We have to understand that we are only little simple men in this world. Only a little wheel in the big hustle of life. That is where we have to do our best and maybe that is where change happens.

As for politics? Oh boy. Sometimes I am tired to think of it. I am too impatient to hear what our Big Men in politics speak but do nothing that I want to beat them with my fists. As for Gorbachev? Perhaps he will change direction. But in general I have no hope that something will change. And what if it does? And the other sides thinks maybe the changes are not so good or not enough? I do not have much hope that they will find the common sense.

…

I had my own friends in Toronto, of course. But there was always something different about my friendship with Frank. Clearly part of the appeal was the exoticism of him being this mysterious foreign presence behind the Iron Curtain. There was also the novelty of his language, which was really just a minor issue. I joked with him often about his English, and there were times when I had trouble understanding him. But it never seemed to matter. I always knew what Frank meant even when I couldn't completely decipher what he'd written.

Letters, of course, have mostly gone the way of the printed newspaper and the record album. Probably no one under the age of thirty has ever composed a letter. I mean, a letter of pen on paper. It's a tangible loss; what we have gained in speed and immediacy we have lost in effort and intimacy.

Often I would frown with frustration puzzling over a mysterious or cryptic passage or phrase in Frank's letters; Frank, too, would have experienced his own frustration. I had enough trouble making myself understood in English, after all, and there he was, trying to make himself understood to me in a foreign language in which he struggled. A paper letter requires a commitment of time and patience. Most importantly, a letter demands our undivided attention in a fashion we don't much see in today's world of instantaneous back-and-forth communications. A letter is a protracted one-way uninterrupted dialogue with the intended recipient. It is, sadly, a lost art.

To be honest, had Frank and I met today and debuted our friendship on email or Skype, I am not sure we would have bonded as deeply.

In many ways, Frank was someone I was both not and longed to be. He was erudite and sophisticated. He travelled widely and was read deeply and across cultures. He smoked a pipe and played the saxophone and read Hemingway and Dostoevsky and visited art galleries and saw Ibsen plays. I admit that I had a hard time reconciling what I imagined life behind the Iron Curtain must be to who Frank was. Why did he seem so interesting and accomplished and so richly fulfilled and I, living amid such comparative luxury in the West, seem so dull and commonplace and…boring? Well, I was not one of those basking in the luxurious life myself!

I was a confused and very average Jew in Toronto. He was a remarkably talented German medical student living behind the Iron Curtain in East Berlin. But he understood me, and I understood him. How the hell could that be?

June 25, 1985
Dear Frank,
I hope that you and your family are well. Please excuse my tardiness in replying to your letters. I hope that in the meantime you did receive my postcards?

I am finally happy in my work, I feel more confidence in myself, more at peace within me. While I was working in men's clothing, I was almost ashamed to be doing that sort of work. Well, with a new "me" it was almost inevitable that I got into a new relationship. I had been avoiding most social contact with women for the past year. Well, I had a couple little flings, but nothing serious. Now, my heart has been opened up for the first time in a long while. It is a good feeling, strange at times though, I'm not used to it. This girl is really crazy about me, and that just wasn't possible a year ago, I mean, I hardly liked myself, why should anyone else?

...

I have noticed that even with the best of intentions, we humans have an amazing capacity for serial self-deception—especially of the inadvertent variety. Looking back, I realized I wanted to sound very upbeat and positive, here. I said I was so happy about my new job. The truth is, it didn't last long. I was truly happy to have met a wonderful girl, but I mentioned almost in passing a line about me having felt unworthy of love.

Why the self-loathing? The self-pity? What was I not facing up to that accounted for such adolescent drama and theatrics? I said I didn't like myself before, so how could anyone else? But then, *she* did.

A new job. A new girlfriend. A new and self-improved Stuart. It was all coming together.

Sometimes, however, it isn't about finding the answers. It's about asking the right questions.

I continued:

> ...This morning I went to synagogue. The rabbi spoke of an uprising against Moses and Aaron by a man named Korach and his allies. Today we would call them "terrorists." In God's fury, there was an earthquake and it devoured the so-called terrorists. So, what does this mean for us?
>
> There will never be unanimous feeling, Frank, always differences, but there are ways to work out differences, rational ways. The Shiites, the Syrians, the members of the PLO (not the Palestinian people) are acting in irrational ways. They feel violence and indiscriminate attacks on civilians is the way to resolve the differences that do exist in the Middle East. I believe that their course of action must change or they will meet with a fate far worse than they can possibly inflict themselves. What really sickened me terribly, was hearing news that the Shiite terrorists singled out Jewish passengers (taking away passengers with Jewish-sounding last names).
>
> Really, Frank, I was shocked that something like this can still happen!
>
> Well, my girlfriend is coming over soon; we will start an early celebration for my twenty-sixth birthday, which is tomorrow.
>
> Until our next correspondence, best wishes to you my friend!
>
> Shalom,
> Stuart

Korach was a powerful Levite and a very important man who, according to Talmudic tradition, convinced a large number of influential allies to join a rebellion against the leadership of Moses and Aaron. God swiftly and summarily put down the rebellion. My point to Frank was that the PLO—a sworn non-Jewish enemy of the State of Israel—needed to be put down and eliminated.

At first it appears as good versus evil, right? Not so fast. It seems Korach's real crime was not that he was evil or greedy, but that he had the audacity—the foolhardy brazenness—to challenge the status quo, or God's will. "Anyone who engages in divisiveness," reads the Talmud, "transgresses a divine prohibition, as it is written: 'And he shall not be as Korach and his company.'"[7]

In fact, his name has become synonymous with "disharmony" and "discord". Is it possible that the real message here is not about the threat from without—the danger posed by your enemy—but the threat from within?

The threat from within is comprised of two components. The first is the internal battle with our self and the second is the internal battle within our own group. The latter: communal disunity. To maintain unity, it seems, requires that the source of disunity be ruthlessly suppressed. And it is only in that unified state where no internal threat exists—no *dissent*—that the threat from without can be successfully defeated.

To be perfectly united means an absolute prohibition on *dissent*.

The risk, of course, is confusing the two: the internal and the external. At the time, it was all too clear to me what the external threat was, and where it was to be found: *the Arabs*, I thought. Again, the question arises about rules and rituals and whether they are a means to an end, or an end in themselves.

I have an acquaintance, a tremendously proud and outspoken Jewish man. He can lapse into what I call a kind of religious triumphalism. To him, the Jews are superior; the smartest, the most accomplished and righteous. But as for the Arabs and Muslims? *"They can't be trusted."* He has attributed far worse adjectives that will not be repeated here. He insists, however, that he does not *hate* them; he hates no one. (Right!!)

"Stuart, look at the facts. Look at history. Look at what they have done. Done to us."

History. The facts. Truth.

Scientists have discovered that we human beings share as much as ninety-seven percent of our DNA with some primates. If we are separated from the primates by only three percent of our DNA, how much biology can separate humans from one another? Biologically speaking, then, we are all the same.

Christians, Jews, and Muslims share essentially the same religious DNA, too; all three believe in the same God. Why so much mutual suspicion and anger? Freud talked about the hostility that can separate the mostly like-minded; he called it the narcissism of small differences. The three monotheistic religions each evolved from the same source—but instead of exploring the bonds that unite us to one another, we push ourselves in the directions of self-isolation and mutual suspicion.

Christians, Jews, Muslims...*us* and *them*. Us *against* them. In time, Catholics would contest with Protestants. Two branches of Islam—Shia and Sunni—wage war against one another over doctrinal issues that to an outsider seem trivial or even meaningless; in my own life, formerly within the orthodox Jewish community, I had participated first-hand in protracted intellectual squabbles over ritualistic minutiae that seem light-years removed from the essential sense of a spiritually informed and meaningful life. How is our religion making us better human beings?

Then again, is it possible it is not the religion's responsibilities, but our own adaptation of it into our lives where the responsibility lies?

Is religion a means to an end, or an end in itself?

I had conversations with friends and colleagues in the religious community about what it means to be a Jew. There is one conversation we don't seem to have enough of: what does it mean to be a human being taking Judaism and its rituals out of that discussion? That is an uncomfortable Spinozian discussion for most.

When it comes to God, maybe the issue is not demanding that we choose a particular following of God, but how to remake ourselves in ways that would be pleasing to God.

* * * *

I am not sure why, but I assumed that most everyone in East Berlin had an avid interest in politics—especially Frank, who had an insatiable passion for it. Frank surprised me. Late in June 1985, he wrote me a letter where he seemed to disavow any interest in politics.

> ...*In this time politics don't move me so hard.*
> *There are other more important problems for me.*
> *I listen every morning to the news from the radio*

and read my daily now and then some words with friends. That's all. It is less important to follow politics then to remain clean and moral in your own life and in your own conscience and to act responsibly and sometimes I think that what in Europe is called civil disobedience could have an important part to play an important role to keep your conscience clean if you want not to accept all what the government or society or the bureaucratic apparatus demands from you. But I'm in doubt that we can see that change much only make some things better....

Erich Fromm was an author Frank would reference in a later letter, and from what I learned of Fromm over time I was not surprised by his influence on Frank. Fromm was a very famous psychotherapist and social theorist who wrote dozens of best-selling books in the fifties and sixties, and was mostly known as a proponent of an enlightened Marxism he called "socialist humanism." Fundamentally, he said that consumption must not be an aim in itself.[8] We all long for a more human, meaningful, and rich life, he said, and socialist humanism was "based on faith in man's ability to build a world which is truly human, in which the enrichment of life and the unfolding of the individual are the prime objects of society, while economics is reduced to its proper role as the means to a humanly richer life."[9]

I knew absolutely nothing of Fromm at this time, and to be honest I am not sure that I would have been at all receptive to his message of socialist humanism. Not at the time. However, the issue of receptivity would come into play at an important part in my life. What I would learn about myself is that often when we think we are being most open, we aren't; in fact, at those moments we can actually be at our most close-minded and intolerant.

> *October 12, 1985*
> *Dear Frank,*
> *Thank you for your postcards from the USSR (CCCP). I told you before that it is so exciting looking for my mail; I never know from which far-off place in the world that I will receive correspondence.*
>
> *I am finally taking a little vacation. I mentioned my girlfriend to you. We really have something beautiful together, though I think it is still too early to be making a lifetime commitment.* [I continued writing about vacationing to Venezuela and the risks of a terrorist incident.]
>
> *We both know that most of these terrorists are Palestinian (PLO) followers of Arafat. They have no respect for the dignity of human life. It sickens me, Frank, I feel that my heart is torn out every time that I see another person killed by their hands. Three Israelis executed in Cyprus, an old, crippled Jewish man tortured and murdered aboard that Italian ship. At least the people of the world can see the true colours of the PLO after such crimes. Even citizens of the CCCP are now being held hostage. Still, they talk in Geneva, Reagan and Gorbachev will talk, many more will talk. At least "talk" does not kill.*
>
> ...

In my letter I mentioned a Jewish passenger who was killed by PLO terrorist.

In 1985, Leon Klinghoffer was a sixty-nine year-old American retiree who was on a thirty-sixth wedding anniversary celebration with his wife on the cruise ship *Achille*

Lauro in Naples. The ship was hijacked by Palestinian terrorists off the coast of Egypt and the terrorists demanded fifty Palestinian prisoners in Israeli jails as ransom. When they were refused docking rights at a Syrian port, the terrorists singled out Klinghoffer, a disabled Jew confined to a wheelchair, and shot him in the head. His body and wheelchair were thrown overboard. It was an outrageous attack. A coldly deliberate callousness, and a barbaric affront to anything human. The Jews in my circle had one word to describe the murderers: "Fuckers."

In Judaism we separate sins against God from sins against our fellow man. Atonement requires first that we seek forgiveness from the person wronged. However, if after repeated efforts we are rebuffed, the wrong is reversed; it is the person who refuses to forgive who wrongs.

Never to forget? If the history of humanity can teach us anything, certainly it is that the best of who we are is the flipside of the worst of who we are; they are inseparable. Let's remember; let us not remember *selectively*. Ultimately it is not a question of who we have been, but who we are determined to be.

What is compassion but a willingness to forgive—or maybe better, to accept or understand? We don't always need to forgive, but understanding is necessary to accept the other perspective. *Us vs. Them* is simply an unwillingness to come to terms with that other person or that other perspective.

Compassion tells us who are we.

I did not disagree with my fellow Jews' vulgar description. The fact is, I told Frank that *"they"* had no respect for "the dignity of human life", but at that time in my life, I will shamefully acknowledge that I felt nothing for the deaths of the Arabs. It is exactly the kind of self-justifying exception that would create so many problems for me in my orthodox life. To dignify human life—if it is to be meaningful—cannot be rationalized.

I remember the fogginess beginning to emerge of not being able to make a distinction at the time between a terrorist and a PLO member, or an unremarkable resident of Gaza, for example. I lumped them all into the same pot. To this day I have acquaintances and friends who tell me there is no difference, primarily because from a young age "they" have been indoctrinated to hate the Jews; and if not actively a participant, "they" turn a blind eye to terrorism.

Nineteen years after the Klinghoffer murder, raw emotions resurfaced in a New York City theatre. It took place in October 2004. Composer John Adams' opera *The Death of Klinghoffer* was about to premier at the Metropolitan in New York City. About one thousand protesters—mostly Jews and many in symbolic wheelchairs—had gathered to protest the opera as anti-Semitic.

One protester said she believed the opera promoted terrorism. "By putting this on a stage in the middle of Manhattan," she told a *Times* reporter, "the message is, 'Go out, murder someone, be a terrorist and we'll write a play about you.'" Ironically, the librettist who wrote the words that so incensed the protester (who admitted she had not seen the opera and had no intention of seeing it), is a Jewish woman named Alice Goodman. Goodman confessed that when the opera debuted back in 1991 she had been quite proud of her work, and was stunned at the abusive response. Her career was ruined and it would be more than twenty years before she received a second commission.[10]

Inside the theatre, meanwhile, a protester at one point leapt to his feet and shouted, "The death of Klinghoffer will never be forgiven."

At one time I would have seconded this sentiment; I would have agreed enthusiastically. I had no wish to forgive. But *never* is a long time.

Metonymy is a figure of speech where a part of the whole comes to stand for the whole. Like calling a banker a "suit", for me, the PLO became shorthand for any Arab.

Despite our very small numbers, we outlasted the empires of the Assyrians, the Babylonians, Persians, Egyptians, the Greeks and the Romans. We somehow survived the Nazis, too. After thousands of years, those predecessor enemies were defeated; but we are still here. It is a compelling observation and one that cannot but instil an almost indescribable pride in the heart of any Jew. And nothing reinforced this Us vs. Them conflict better than the Arab attacks against Israel. Or against Jews anywhere in the world.

It almost didn't matter what the circumstances might have been. A Jew was attacked. That was all that mattered to us. And who was to blame? *Them!*

At that point in my life I'm not sure I had completely inculcated this feeling, but I was headed in that mental fixation. I was not comfortable with the rhetorical extremes of Zionism, but my sense of common cause with Israel and its fight against its enemies was emergent. In my letter to Frank I am surprised that I was still on the high road. But I was definitely striking more aggressive tones. The low road was coming into view. I could feel it.

What was developing in my mind quite forcefully was a distinct ideology of Us vs. Them. Overtime, this distinction would take up a larger and ever-increasing percentage of my mindset. But the seeds really took to soil at the time of the PLO terrorist attacks. I saw the signs. More and more I was with my fellows on the low road. Israel was the hapless victim and the Arabs were the aggressors. Like my black-and-white East Berlin, the conflict between the Jewish people and the Arabs was crystallizing in my mind. *They are the enemy; there are no distinctions.*

About ten years later, in 1994, an American-born Jew by the name of Baruch Goldstein murdered twenty-nine Palestinian people at a prayer service in Hebron, a flashpoint city about thirty miles south of Jerusalem. Known as the Cave of the Patriarchs massacre, an additional 125 Islamic worshippers were wounded in the attack.

The Israeli government instinctively condemned the attack, but even so, Goldstein became something of a hero to many. I felt shame and shock for his actions; what I don't remember feeling was simple and basic outrage or sadness on behalf of the innocent victims. To me, there were no innocent victims—that was how deep the idea of the "enemy" was taking hold of me. It had been a public relations blunder. That Arabs had died—that there could be such a thing as innocent Arabs—was less and less real to me. All I saw was *us* and *them.*

For me, anti-Semitism was no longer a problem "over there"; it had ceased to be an abstraction; it had become personal. An attack on the Jews—any Jew—was an attack on all Jews. And an attack on me.

At this point in 1985, my religious indoctrination had begun. Yet, I would not take the decisive plunge or commitment for several more years. What I was feeling at this time was that I was a Jew in that obsessive, all-consuming self-identification sense, and I was feeling threatened for the first time in my life. *Us vs. Them* felt extremely real and immediate to me.

CHAPTER 6

GERMAN KNIVES

> What may appear as truth to one person will often appear as untruth to another person. But that need not worry the seeker. Truth and untruth often coexist; good and evil often are found together.
> —Mahatma Gandhi

In our letters, Frank and I often still assessed and positioned our view of the world from the vantage point of what we were individually familiar with. The push and pull of the Cold War propelled us both to attempt to put forth our parochial interpretation while we simultaneously attempted to see the other side, and mostly in order as not to offend.

April 20, 1986
Dear Frank,
I hope you are well.
I find myself remembering something you said to me in Berlin. You told me that you are more knowledgeable about politics of international significance because you, unlike myself, can listen to

the news of the East and the West. You can take all the bullshit and come up with your own conclusions. I, on the other hand, only have Western B.S. to listen to. Still, from our perspective it appears quite clear that Libya does encourage, support and promote terrorism worldwide. I fully understand that one man's terrorist is another's freedom fighter, but it seems as though Col. Qaddafi has gone beyond this distinction. [...]

You mentioned in your last letter the incident in Cairo, well, it appears that these senseless and random killings of innocents is supported mainly by Syria, Iran and Libya. Frank, I realize that these statements are basically Western thought, but I would be very interested to hear your point of view, objectively, on this subject. You know I am usually against what Reagan and his administration stand for, but I have to say I fully support the bombing of Libya. I feel that the world should have learned a lesson over a policy of appeasement; slowly, the USA may be coming around. It doesn't matter if the bomb in Berlin (FRG) wasn't committed by Libyans, the USA didn't respond to any one particular offense, but to a general policy of terrorism anywhere and everywhere carried out many, many times by Libya.

Speaking of seeing the news from East and West, this accident must have seemed like two different events, depending on which news report you were listening to. One report would say hundreds killed, the next thousands, another would say that a total meltdown occurred... Talk about propaganda.

...

At that point I told Frank that the recent nuclear meltdown at Three Mile Island in Pennsylvania in late March of that year could have been a kind of poetic justice for the nuclear disaster at Chernobyl—almost exactly one year prior. I made the (not very original) point that the contest between the two superpowers could have reached a level where it was not about ideology anymore, but ego. It was like a fight between two drunks. It seemed as though no one knew what it was about since no one could remember how it started in the first place, and both were so plastered their punches couldn't knock over a tin can. However, what I didn't realize was how many empty punches I was throwing in this interminable rivalry of *Us vs. Them*.

I accused the Americans of not being objective. Then again, pure propaganda does not present as objectivity, especially to the outsider. In the geopolitical sphere, propaganda is often intended for domestic audience consumption. How do we know if we are being objective in our personal interactions when the audience and judge of that objectivity must then be our own authentic self?

Deep down, we always know. Is it possible to be just objective enough?

> *...You know, commies in Cuba, Nicaragua, and El Salvador are perceived to be a direct threat, whether we are talking about the people in the Kremlin or in and around Moscow, there seems to be no perceived difference in the general mind of many Americans. That is what really scares me, and in my mind it has surfaced in the aftermath of Chernobyl. Some form of constructive dialogue must take place within America itself to amend the*

situation as I see it, and I don't mean that Americans should become naïve, but they become a little more objective in thought.

As you can see, Frank, I can get carried away sometimes.

I know that one day we will meet again, it just wasn't in the cards this time, especially financially. I've been spending too much, and not earning enough lately.

Take care,
Stuart

This was an interesting letter mostly from what was omitted from our discussion.

A week earlier, the United States authorized airstrikes against Libya in retaliation for what it claimed was Col. Gadhafi's involvement in a shocking terrorist bombing of a discothèque in West Berlin on April 5. The club, *La Belle*, was a well-known hangout popular to American servicemen. Three people were killed—two of them American servicemen—and almost 250 injured—many of whom lost limbs.

What I did not address directly but was on my mind—and surely must have been on Frank's mind, as well—was that the smoking gun US president Reagan used for justifying the air strike on Libya had been an intercepted telex from East Berlin shortly after the attack, congratulating Gadhafi on a "job well done."[11]

The retributory American attack on Libya killed forty people, one of whom purportedly was Gadhafi's adopted infant daughter. At the time, like many armchair apologists of Realpolitik, I believed the action necessary and the consequences in terms of casualties regrettable, but acceptable.

Many years later, I would meet Dr. Izzeldin Abuelaish and would come to a very different conclusion about the "acceptable expendability" or collateral damage of human life in times of war.

I am in no means linking the brutal Libyan dictator Gadhafi and his actions to the wonderful Palestinian humanitarian and advocate for peace, Dr. Abuelaish.

I had mixed feelings about President Ronald Reagan. Like many Canadians, I was skeptical of his simplistic and reductionist reference to the Soviet Union in 1983 as the "Evil Empire"—words that would echo down the corridor of history to 2012 when George W. Bush famously branded North Korea, Iraq and Iran the "Axis of Evil". On the other side of the scale, Reagan's seemingly complicated scheme to funnel money to the contras in Nicaragua, which became known as the Iran-Contra Affair, struck me as hubris and overreach. Why did the American people think the solution to every world problem was America itself? And what did the Soviet people think of that posturing? That the Americans were part of the "Axis of Good"? Isn't it simply an alternative perspective?

On the other hand, Gadhafi was firmly anti-Israel. He had supported anti-Israel organizations in the Palestinian territories, in Syria and—in a development depressingly reminiscent of events today with Iran and North Korea—supposedly was anxious to develop Libya's own nuclear program.

In this last letter, I was not yet exhibiting my own rigid perspective as to be insensitive to offending Frank; I was always aware of our unique relationship, of being a NATO-based Jew possibly intruding into his communist and German world—and fearing that if I ever did offend him enough, it would be quite easy for him to say, "That is enough, it was fun while it lasted." I think I was trying to be honest and careful in my assessments, mostly doing my best to be objective. Yet, is it not subjectivity that one possesses by seeing things from only one perspective?

I watched Saddam's hanging on TV in 2006. I was not jubilant, nor was I particularly traumatized. I think by that time I was a bit numb about the fate awaiting him inside the world of absolute dictatorships. His conviction and execution was celebrated by many as a triumph for the West. Good versus evil; *us against them*. We were the good guys, of course. The same kind of morbid euphoria broke out in 2011 when Osama bin Laden was killed in his home in Afghanistan by a detachment of elite American Marines. And I certainly would never defend a man like Osama bin Laden. But even evil has a perspective.

There was a media storm of outrage just a week after the 9/11 attacks when the American talk show host Bill Maher of *Politically Incorrect* complained about the suicide bombers of 9/11 being labeled as cowards. Was it cowardly, he asked rhetorically, for zealots to commandeer and steer an airplane into a building, knowing it meant certain death? Yes, they were misguided. They may have been brainwashed. Yes, their strategy was barbaric. But did they act cowardly?

What happens in the world is interpretable and how we interpret what happens is heavily conditioned by ritual. For instance, 9/11 immediately became a Good Guy versus Bad Guy scenario: Us vs. Them. Conversely, the Oklahoma City bombing in 1995 turned out to be a much more complex narrative. This time there was no convenient "them" to play the role of Bad Guy. Not at first, anyway.

In my letter I inferred that the American administration lacked objectivity. As a Canadian I believe I was like many who worried about the US perspective that tended to habitually confuse might with right. I was working very hard in that letter to be objective with Frank.

What is not clear to me now (and what I am not sure was clear to me then, either) was whether or not *objectivity* was authentic. Did I really feel the way I expressed? Or was I playing a role for Frank by hiding my truer emotions that were slowly becoming inflamed and exacerbated by events in the Middle East? Was it more important to be honest, or to be seen by Frank as being honest in a way that would reflect well on me?

The point is, at the time and given my deepening subjectivity concerning the Arab-Jewish conflict, I was not sure I *really* did fault the American administration for its lack of "objectivity".

The Arab–Jewish conflict began to weigh heavily on my global geopolitical outlook. I complained that world leaders were forcing the narrative of the world's problems into a simple black and white, right or wrong, *us and them* categorization. "It's wrong," I said. What I could not have admitted to myself at the time, however, was that I did not likely believe it. Maybe it was *us against them?* If by "us", of course, you meant the Jews. We often try to raise the bar of alarm with the analogy of the canary in the coalmine warning—first the Jews, and then you…

I next heard from Frank in June. He was jubilant because he had a new girlfriend. I had been planning a trip to England and Frank wished me well, but expressed his disappointment that I wouldn't have time to visit him on the European continent. He said he would have enjoyed showing me the sights again. He wrote some more about his new girlfriend and how wonderful she was and how lucky he was, and then I could almost hear him take a deep calming breath as he switched gears.

> ...You wrote a lot about the terrorism problem and the bombing of Libya. You know that terrorism is no way to solve political problems. And often on the contrary they only infuriate their enemies. But I find it necessary to find in policy other ways or possibilities. As it said in the old Bible, an eye for an eye and a tooth for a tooth. It's too dangerous today. It can't be that kind of policy for the end of the twentieth century.
>
> Of course Colonel Gaddafi is a terrible dictator. But in policy we have to find another language other than weapons. We have to learn to see our own behaviour as a cause and a reason and an effect or a result—a consequence and also the behaviour of our opposite. We simply have to understand all communication as a circular process. And not like the time to see only one side our behaviour as the result of doing from the opposite. You say yourself that one man's terrorist is another man's freedom fighter. And of course there are strong interests in policy and political power and the economy.
>
> It frightened me to hear that a lot of Americans agreed uncritically with Reagan's decision to bomb Libya. That makes me suspicious if so much people need it to take their pride from identification if they can identify with such abstract things like their nation their fatherland like the power of USA like such an action of their government to get by that way

> *pleasure, particularly if that are such military actions against other people or people died. Particularly we in Germany are sensitive to such things. We think to our history. To what has happened with fascism. I think you understand what I mean.*
>
> *...*

I read that letter embarrassingly. He probably thought I was "one of those Americans" who felt President Reagan did what had to be done. It pained me to know that Frank saw that in my letter, yet chose not to confront me on it. He fed me a lifeline, "I think you understand what I mean."

I was very happy clinging to the rhetorical podium with both hands and also to have the pot constantly on a rolling boil. Frank was always about the simmer. I laugh at my tone now. Frank was becoming a friend, one who saw past my faults and focused on that uncanny, unexplainable connection that friends have. Lucky for me.

What surprised me, too, was that Frank seemed to be taking a distinctly non-ideological line.

What kind of Communist was he? He sounded so reasonable and non-doctrinaire. Instead of aping the party line about the superiority of the communist system, he seemed to be attacking all ideology. He was far more "objective" than I, which was startling given that he had far more reason than I to be biased. After all, wasn't he the one living under an authoritarian regime that hid the "truth" from its people? And me, the one flourishing in the open and free society?

Frank mentioned the Americans and what he perceived as their ideological chauvinism directly, but indirectly indicted the poisonous hubris of German history, as well. It was particularly interesting to me that he deliberately shaded his meaning at the end of the letter and left me to fill in the blanks. I would learn years later that this technique was his modus operandi. Frank referred to it as a kind of double-entry bookkeeping: we talk one way with our closest friends, but speak in an entirely different way with those outside the inner circle. I took this as a compliment.

Years later, we would talk about it in more detail.

> *June 23, 1986*
> *Dear Stuart,*
> *In our last letters we talked about politics in South Africa. But I think we need to ask what we can do in our own little daily world and how we can show responsibility in local political things. We should act ourselves in our own immediate environment. I must say that I am not active enough. As a student I was mostly concentrating on studies. On the other side I am dealing with a good life. Cultural things, friends. So in life what can the little man on the street do. I want to think more about that and will write about it later. What do you think?*
> *All the best,*
> *Frank*

The theme of this short letter concerning "the little man on the street" has shaped a considerable amount of my evolved and current perspective on matters about the world. Frank at the time as a Communist East German and me a Western Jew, unintentionally at the time took matters into our own hands and forged a relationship, initially through openness and curiosity, that epitomized Frank's question about what the little man can accomplish. A lot, I think. A lot.

August 17, 1986
Dear Frank,
We have been talking about getting married next summer. Nothing official. I haven't even officially been down on one knee to ask her. I'm just waiting for the right moment, I think that is it, it seems right. I just get very queasy about marriage, my parents are divorced when I was 13 years old, and I see it all around me. Is divorce a problem in the DDR? Almost half of all marriages end in divorce. I am just afraid of being a statistic.

...

I discussed the possibility of getting married, and instead of joy I confessed to Frank I was mostly worried about ending up as a statistic as my parents did—and my father's parents, too! *They say things happen in threes.* I quickly segued from the personal to the political.

...Frank, I have great difficulty in categorizing you and I as "us" and "them". It is a sickening reality that is created by governments, not by people like you and me. It makes me wonder what those people in government are made of. Are they different from us in some way? I have the answer! If we could get a few hundred million people—half from the USA and NATO and half from the USSR and Warsaw Pact nations—to write letters to each other, as we do, and then arrange an exchange of these people for a week or so...

That's it! All we need now is organization. Do you suppose that the UN could be put to some good use? Think about it; it could mean a joint Nobel Peace Prize for us....

I was joking, of course. But it was the kind of whimsical and silly notion that was routinely dismissed as naïve and impractical, but that could actually work—"...*the little man on the street.*" And the reason it might have worked was just because so many pundits scoffed that it wouldn't. Perhaps it is not too late.

> *November 8, 1986*
> *Dear Frank,*
> *I hope you are well.*
> *This marriage business is good. We have been living together now for one year and it has been great. We completely complement one another; we are growing together, learning together and truly loving each other. Even though life promises no guarantees, we both feel extremely confident about our relationship. I know that I told you that we don't fight, but we have had difficult moments, more so the result of my difficulties and work and career concerns. We come out of it stronger and more committed to one another than before. I hope that you can realize such feelings with your girlfriend. It is a great feeling to be so secure in a relationship as I am.*
> *Well that is all for now. Keep well and enjoy!*
> *Your friend,*
> *Stuart*

Frank had a funny quote about marriage: marriage is the effort by two people to solve problems, which you never had alone.

My parents fought and their arguments were mostly about money. With my father travelling so much and to such exotic places, I had assumed he was doing well financially. He wasn't. It was always a struggle even at the best of times.

I told Frank that my girlfriend and I never fought. That seemed a very positive sign to me. It probably would have been a better thing if we had a few small occasional skirmishes. At least we would have learned how to better air our eventual disagreements. Otherwise, bad feelings just fester and harden. We never did learn how to fight. What I eventually discovered about relationships is that both parties need to evolve and allow growth, not to resist change, listen to each other, check your ego at the door…and you have to be willing to take risks—to fail and recommit. Unfortunately, I had only my parents' marriage as a template.

Talking of wedding plans, I acknowledge that the few problems that my wife to be and I were experiencing were my own issues. I thought I had managed my fears about my own parents' situation and the statistics on divorce. Not exactly the gushy optimism one might expect from a young man on the threshold of bliss. Still, I did sound very happy about our plans. It seems like such a long time ago.

I do recall a rather awkward fight we had (or was it just a difference of perspective?) when we registered for our wedding gifts. It was the first serious disagreement we had. We were adding to our registry many small kitchen items and appliances, such as coffee makers and pots and pans and ice cream makers, mixers and assorted kitchen gadgets that I had never heard of. She picked out a beautiful set of cutlery she really loved. It was actually quite attractive—very modern, but functional. Then I noticed the MADE IN WEST GERMANY label. I turned her down flat. "No. We aren't getting these."

"You said you loved them."

"It doesn't matter. Absolutely not. No way. I am not going to have anything made in Germany in my house. I'm not going to spend the rest of my life using German knives."

I shot her a, "You know, the Germans? The ones who orchestrated the Holocaust?" look.

"That's ridiculous. I like them."

I was shocked. Up until that point, we were on common ground in this area; maybe she was not as knee-jerk anti-German as I, but I thought we were at least in the same chapter, if not on the same page. It bothered me that she could compromise the principles I thought she had simply because she "liked" the cutlery. There were many other sets of cutlery to choose from.

It was ridiculous, of course. It was stupid. I lost that battle.

> *August 7, 1987*
> *Dear Frank,*
> *The wedding approaches. I still have to prepare my speech. I'm afraid I may get emotional, so I want to have it memorized. We are going to Yugoslavia for our honeymoon, to a little seaside resort....*

Two months earlier, on June 12, President Reagan travelled to West Berlin to mark the city's 750th anniversary. Not surprisingly, it was not the past he focused on, but the immediate future. Appearing in front of a large crowd at the Brandenburg Gate, Reagan famously challenged his Soviet counterpart Mikhail Gorbachev to "tear down this wall."

At the time, I assumed the speech was less of a pragmatic suggestion than a needling tweak by the American president. I thought what we all probably thought: *There is no way in hell that wall is coming down.* It was, however, around this time that we in the West began hearing unfamiliar phrases filtering out from Moscow such as *glasnost* and *perestroika*. (This was the first time, by the way, that I risked admitting to Frank in print that I had worked at Xerox. Opportunistically, I had left Xerox before the wedding, so it felt safe at that point!)

We were married August 23, 1987. It was one of the happiest days I can remember.

Frank was an invited guest, receiving the same fancy and personalized invitation that all our other guests received—without the "stamped" R.S.V.P. card. I never expected that he would be permitted to leave East Germany for a Jewish wedding in Canada, but I really wanted him there. It would have meant so much to me. We managed to include him in the festivities.

> *November 28, 1987*
> *Dear Frank,*
> *Many apologies for not having written as of late.*
> *The wedding was beautiful. Your letter that reached us expressing your best wishes was read out to the guests at the reception by my wife's brother, and it was definitely one of the highlights of the day. […]*
> *Intellectually, I am getting a lot out of synagogue. I go every Saturday and thoroughly enjoy it. One aspect of it is very moving, when there is a moment of thought for the Jews of the Soviet Union. There is a chair by the rabbi that is always left empty as a symbol of protest for the Jewish families who wish to leave the USSR but cannot.*

> [...] *I understand that you are now a real doctor! Sincere congratulations!! You should be very proud of your accomplishment.*
>
> *All the best to you my good friend,*
> *Stuart*

I had transitioned into marriage with dreams of a hopeful future, personal joy and emotional stability, yet I was going down a path that I was indoctrinating with an increasingly rigid and resolute mindset.

CHAPTER 7

US VS. THEM

> Freedom would be not to choose between black
> and white but to abjure such prescribed choices.
> —Theodor Adorno

Despite the one-time confident predictions of Frank's Karl Marx, a Communist regime would not result in revolution of the proletarian and the establishment of a worker's paradise—at least not thus far in history.

By the 1980s the Soviet Union was decomposing from the inside out. Its economy had stalled, its agriculture and technology sectors were seriously underperforming, antiquated factories were producing third-rate merchandise no one really wanted, and people were in a rebellious mood after nearly seven decades of strict authoritarian control and economic stagnation. The only sign of prowess emanating from the USSR was their potent military machine and their domination of international athletics.

In an effort to relieve some of the built-up economic and social tension, Mikhail Gorbachev introduced a series of modest reforms (*perestroika*) and dubbed the new spirit *glasnost*, meaning "openness."

Freedom! It was what everyone had been dreaming of, and it seemed too good to be true. Through July to September I received three exuberant postcards from Frank, who was travelling in the Soviet Union. Huge and dramatic changes were in the air and on the street!

> *July 12, 1988*
>
> *Greetings from this fine city. Leningrad! Much museums, galleries, art. Leningrad is the city of Peter I (the Great). Second it is the city of Lenin, the leader of the Russian Revolution. And this revolution is still all alive here. Wherever you go you find places of life and what they are doing. A lot of history. It simply is a place that has to be visited.*
>
> *Thank you for your last card.*
> *Frank*
>
>
> *July 18, 1988*
>
> *In front of the Hermitage. On the street you can hear some of perestroika. On the main street late in the night. Lots of musicians, artists and singers. Last night we saw a modern ballet. I have never seen such a ballet. I think in general the Soviet Union would be very interesting for you.*
> *Frank*

> *September 6, 1988*
> *All my best wishes for a Happy New Year 1988, with this photograph, a postcard of mine, I made it in the USSR.*
> *"For glasnost ready? Ever ready!"*
> *You see Christine as a young pioneer with my pipe in her mouth as she reports "Ever ready!"*
> *All my best,*
> *Frank*

So much has happened since that time—so much has changed—that I am not sure I can convey in words the feeling of buoyant and almost childish optimism that Frank must have felt with the first inklings of *glasnost*. I know I felt that way. I was so happy for him. To be honest, however, I had my doubts, too. How far would it go? How long would it last? Could things really change that much?

I followed the news and political developments as it pertained to the Soviet Union and its satellites in the Communist East with great enthusiasm. Could this be possible? Was *perestroika* for real? Frank's cards and letters seemed to suggest it was. I wasn't so sure. After all, the Soviet system had been in place and uncontested since 1917. Certainly it would take more than a few street artists and musicians to topple one of the world's most repressive, powerful, yet indomitable political regimes…?

Wouldn't it?

I next heard from Frank in October 1988. He told me that he and his girlfriend were moving in together. Despite that good personal news, their trip to the Eastern Bloc country of Romania to visit friends dampened his tone. He was struck by the poverty he witnessed there combined with the absence of any changing political winds. His mood was a bit less enthusiastic about *glasnost* and *perestroika*.

> ...But about in general this country there is nothing spectacular to say. People who still wait for perestroika from the government side. Nothing glasnost. The same like in GDR where it is all this old man dominate in policy. Nothing changes.
>
> We visited Romania to see friends and saw their big poverty as never before. The most German and Hungarian people try to leave their country which is very difficult. People which still remain behind are despairing and resigned. It's a deep feeling especially to come to this country. You get a depressive feeling. Suddenly you get into a rage to see all that and understand some of the same mechanisms in our country.
>
> ...

He still sounded confident that change would come—that it was inevitable. However, in that letter I detected the first hint from Frank that reform—*true* reform—might have been a far more difficult undertaking than people like me might have assumed.

> **October 4, 1988**
> Dear Stuart,
>
> Too much work at first, but that is my life at the moment at the hospital. I just try to write the examination but am too tired. I haven't slept enough. Some of my colleagues are on holiday and I work over the summer.
>
> Our visit in Leningrad was really interesting. A good opportunity to see and hear what people are thinking and feeling about the new way of

feeling—glasnost and perestroika. I can say that glasnost is practised. We have seen it on the streets, in the papers and in TV and now in talks with the people. They speak free about important problems in society. But you have to understand that glasnost is only one problem. It's only the supposition for the perestroika of the society in economical and political things. Perestroika is the real problem; it is much more difficult and need surely a lot of time. Here will the future show how things can really change life to make the socialism again attractive, as Gorbachev said.

For me, for us in the GDR, it is more important how this ideas can be realized in our country. And that is the problem. Our government is still against glasnost. But people on the base discuss much about that.

...

Frank saw the contrast between the important, but mostly modest openness of *glasnost* and the deep (perhaps intractable) systemic structural problems preventing *perestroika* that characterized life in the GDR. What really struck me, though—and quite frankly, surprised me—was his comment that he hoped Gorbachev's reforms would *improve* and *sustain* socialism rather than replace it.

As a capitalist living in one of the freest and most economically successful (or is it stressful?) countries in the world, it was hard for me to imagine what it could be about socialism that *still* enchanted him. Surely he saw its defeat as a clear referendum on the unconditional superiority of capitalism?

Perhaps Frank would say that he was hoping for reform *to something* and not just reform *from something*. What good is freedom if, when viewed this way, merely liberates more of what ultimately destroys us? Is freedom the ability to vote in a free, open and fair election? Is freedom the opportunity to travel anywhere in the world? Is freedom the right to live with someone who also wants to live with you? What good is freedom if it is merely the opportunity of purchasing a luxury automobile, but the majority forever lacking the funds to do so? And is freedom the opportunity to be destroyed by capitalistic greed? I think Frank was still hoping that eventual change would allow East German society to thrive in a free, but still socialistic, political order.

I do believe that in our search for truth—*our* truth—we are seeking that elusive peace and balance in our lives, regardless of where we live. After all, the West has its truth and the East has its truth. And *truth*, just like the rituals we embrace, is just another commodity that we protect at all costs.

Adam Smith warned us not to confuse self-interest with selfishness.[12] Self-interest cannot be only what benefits *me*— but what benefits *us*. Selfishness is what benefits *only me*. I am quite sure Frank knew and understood this even thirty years ago. I saw Communism, for instance, only for what it wasn't. It was hard for me to imagine a downside to the fall of Communism. But of course, I was speaking as one fully indoctrinated into Western ideology and its mindset and rituals.

I drank the Kool-Aid. Only, in my case it was the flavour of Westernism. I was brainwashed. Our biases, whatever they may be and from wherever they emanated, are hard to relinquish. Our bias is not *our* truth; it can be someone else's.

It occurs to me today that Frank came to his own understanding from two completely separate and incommensurable sources: the East and the West ("You only get the bullshit from the Western media. I get the bullshit from the Western media *and* the Eastern media..."). Throughout the majority of his lifetime, Frank had been landlocked in the East, but remarkably exposed to the West in a historically unique fashion. It may be possible that living amongst two opposed biases permitted one as aware as Frank to reach the conclusion that one bias could be *right* and the other could be *wrong*, but maybe that both are wrong. Or that both are right—a third perspective.

Frank was also seeing firsthand the pending collapse of the Soviet Empire, which contributed far more to his enlightenment than to mine. Only he had what I perceived as this authentic perspective on both systems, and the really interesting thing about that was his suggestion in his letters: that the truth was not one or the other, but maybe this *third* perspective—a perspective that united what worked in both systems and discarded what didn't. What if religions were like that?

I had an analogous experience in my own religious odyssey. How enlightening it was to participate in two polar opposite worlds (at different periods of my life) and coming to the understanding of the opposite perspective. I'd like to think that the final result of this odyssey was that consummate third perspective that Frank possessed. To be clear, I went from a secular Jew to a religious Jew, and then leaving the religious world to partake in that third perspective.

This seems to be the kind of meaning-making that Rabbi Sacks recommended. But it means the risk of abandoning cherished habits of belief and outdated rituals. For instance, what if Jews, Christians and Muslims and all faiths and non-faiths all agreed to renounce violence and war? Naïve? Sure, maybe it is. At this point in time it surely was—for me.

But nothing that can be imagined is impossible. Unfortunately, I wasn't yet imagining peace between the Arabs and Israelis. I had more to learn from Frank.

> *October 24, 1988*
> Dear Frank,
> As I see it, the tougher things get, the more violence by the Arabs; unfortunately, the more aggressive the Israelis must become. It may or may not ever end, but if Israel gives in and ends the "iron fist" policy, the Arabs will smell blood and go for the kill. I am afraid for Israel's security if Peres and the Labour Peaceniks win. It doesn't look like they will.
> ...
>
> *January 1, 1989*
> Dear Stuart,
> Thank you for your last long and informative letter. I hope all is well with you in the New Year. Excuse this short words, no time, have to serve in the army for three months February-April, as do all: Then you will hear more from me. Much happens and change, more inside than out.
> Your friend,
> Frank

Frank was avoiding a conflicting response to my last letter regarding Israel and her bellicose neighbours. He finally made the time to address it—but only after he began on the simmer first.

February 23, 1989
Dear Stuart,
Meanwhile you got some of my postcards from Czechoslovakia on which I promised to write a longer letter. Today I begin with that promise. At first thank you for your last letter. It's a long time ago and I'm only remembering some things you wrote about your new flat and plans.

For four weeks I do service in the army as a doctor, here in a little city in the northeast of the country near Polish border. Still eight weeks. It's a boring job, not so much to work, a lot of young healthy men which don't want to be here and become "ill" if they don't want to make their service. Can you imagine how senseless and foolish it is? Simple pathological. Real, we need disarmament. But enough from that.

I'm again, after three years, an alone-living man. I divorce from her or better divided. To explain it would need hours, it's too complicated. I didn't want it and after all this trouble I hoped we could find a new beginning together—but she didn't want a new start. That is the fact. At the beginning of the year I felt very mad and sad; it hurt's me very much. I went through the "valley of tears." A sad and deep emotional experience.

Later I began to understand that the parting from her meant for me more than only the parting from her. I experienced now a new kind of "to be alone" of oneself/myself; real alone is a deeper meaning as understood before. And I know it, this experience was real high necessary for me to have. I have it still and live with a new higher self-responsibility, where is no one in the background, no security. It means to find real alone my own way of life. [...]

Recently I read from Ingmar Bergman "Scenes of a Marriage". (The film I saw many years ago) which I want to recommend you read/or see. There I found some of my problems with my girlfriend; in general I would say this story's contents and shows some dangers and risks of a partnership.

...

Frank was in a melancholy mood and his dark thoughts about his recent separation were not made sunnier by the prospect of mandatory army service. I was shocked yet naïve to discover that soldiers routinely faked illnesses or improvised injuries to be cashiered from service. He asked, "What about politics?" I could almost hear him sighing.

I was taken aback by his uncharacteristically bleak and almost despairing tone. Then again, I had never been much of an Ingmar Bergman fan. Leave it to Frank to calm his broken heart by seeing a downbeat film about relationships from the cinematic master of gloom and annihilating despair. Anyway, what about politics?

...As you can understand it involves me very few. In GDR is all the same. Our society is, I would say, simple neurotic. And neurotic means mendacious, lazy, cowardly. So I read no paper, listen on radio, look no TV (rarely the programs from the West). From government side there is no sincerity only bad made ideology, and that I know already too long.

And international? I think it would be good if Israel come with PLO on one table to speak together. To give the Palestinian people proof for their own country-state. I think is necessary to make an end with the conflict. People have to speak together and reach for a good agreement for a peaceful common way of life. There is no other possibility and it needs the readiness of both sides to find this way. Gorbachev show's today this readiness, but from the west comes not enough.

For today enough. You will hear again from me. Let me hear something from your daily life and your thinking.

All my best wishes,
Frank

Even sunken in a personal gloom, Frank still managed to strike a note of sensible optimism about the international order and a reasonable and humane approach. Conflict must be avoided. He expressed confidence that Gorbachev was not only ready, but willing. It was up to the West to reciprocate.

By this time, Ronald Reagan had left office. His then Vice President, George H. W. Bush, had succeeded him and it was President Bush who would preside over the forthcoming seismic changes that were to take place.

March 10, 1989
Dear Frank,
I am sick at home trying to get rid of this flu. So, I also have time to reply to your last letter. I don't know where to begin. I have never received a letter from you that seemed to be as disturbing as this one was. Instead of disturbing, I could say depressing, negative, even searching.

> As an army doctor, you said you saw healthy young men "getting sick" in order to be relieved of service, and that the army is senseless, so therefore we need disarmament. Then, the very sad news about your separation from your girlfriend…
>
> These are sentiments which I do not believe I have heard from you before. Your solution to the problems of the Middle East I would respectfully say are naïve, but more directly you seem to be fed up with the whole solution so you give me a perceived easy solution.
>
> …

I can see now the level of difficulty I was having responding to his letter. I cannot believe how aggressively tactless I was being to Frank. But wait, there's more.

> …I am not a trained psychologist, but I wonder if you are trying to tell me something, or even to convince yourself of something, of some course of action or direction.
>
> …

"Not a trained psychologist, but…"? Okay, so not only was I obnoxiously condescending, but insensitive. It had been my experience that in dark moments, one appreciates nothing quite so much as amateur psychoanalysis—especially when the person suffering is himself a trained psychotherapeutic professional. Lucky for Frank, he had me and my infinite wisdom and experience!

> …In your letter is an outpouring of emotion and not just from the breakup of a relationship. My experiences of an ended relationship were also at the time very difficult, however, they occurred when I was much younger and certainly not as emotionally

mature as you or I would be today. I hate to even consider what it could be like if that were to happen between my wife and me.

...

"Hey, Frank, sorry to hear about your devastating breakup. But here's some good news: it didn't happen to me!" (Sadly, I would find out exactly what it was like and especially the loneliness that would ensue.)

...You know something, aside from this last letter, I have always envied you, though not in a jealous way; it is just that you always seemed to have such a rich and full life. You are part of an esteemed profession, you are cultured, you travel frequently and if you don't mind my saying this, you appear to be of a privileged group (I shouldn't use the word "class" in a Marxist state). For all the problems of the GDR, you don't seem to be doing too badly.

...

I might also have been taking a jab at Frank and the socialist experiment by making the bold proposition that he may have belonged to a privileged class, something abhorrent in a "pure and wholesome" Marxist state. My only hope at this point was that Frank's command of English was even worse than he suggested, or as a doctor recognized the negative repercussions the flu was having on my common sense. On this personal matter, looking back, I either had an off day having been under the weather, my mind was elsewhere, or I really wanted to get to the politics of the letter and I rushed through the personal stuff. I am not sure. Anyway, the letter continued at some length and of course segued yet again into politics. I complained to Frank rather bitterly that even in the USA where there was a large population of Jews, it was hard to find "balanced" reporting on Israel. And of course, by balanced I meant pro-Israel.

I complained about a local newspaper I—and other Jews—would not buy because of its perceived anti-Israeli prejudice. Had it been 2017 I might have even proclaimed that the phenomenon of fake news was at play! I said that the biggest problem for Israel was its free press. Reporters were free to report on the truth and unfortunately that meant sometimes reporting on some ugly facts. But the "other side" only allowed reporters access to staged propaganda that flattered the Palestinian cause.

I asked Frank if we could trust the PLO. Could we trust Arafat? Could we trust any Palestinian? (I did indeed sound very much like that friend of mine I criticized earlier who insisted he hated no one.)

> …Did you know that while Arafat has recognized Israel's right to exist and renounced terrorism to a non-Arabic press, in Arabic he has never renounced anything and even refuted those remarks?…

And the answer to those questions would be a big fat, "No."

> …How does a leopard change his spots so quickly? How do you react to an enemy who has vowed to destroy you? Why is the world so willing to believe him? Do you realize the threat to Israel that the PLO in the name of Palestine would cause? Can you fathom it? How can we believe that the PLO's intention is not to wipe Israel off the face of the earth? The PLO still has not changed their charter, in which it states their desire to destroy the state of Israel. If they do want peace, why don't they do something about this?…

Not unreasonable questions. What I was putting forth, however, was the monologue and not the dialogue. The Jewish philosopher Martin Buber said that a critical point in a relationship occurred when it went from *I—Thou* to *I—to It*. Basically, the "Thou" that recognized the humanity of the "Other" (the You and the Me) was relegated to the dehumanized status of a *Thing*. The *"It"*.[13]

> ...Until the "others" can understand this, and try and see things from the Israeli side, then a settlement is out of the question.
>
> ...

Us vs. Them was shifting into high gear.

Naturally by "others" I meant Buber's *It*—anyone who didn't agree with me that my perspective and that of my ideological soul mates in the Jewish community was the truth. The American politician Barry Goldwater made a famous (some say infamous) statement when accepting the 1964 presidential nomination. He said, "I would remind you that extremism in the defence of liberty is no vice! And let me remind you also that moderation in the pursuit of justice is no virtue!"[14] That the senator would be criticized during the campaign for apparently supporting nuclear strikes on Vietnam should have led one to wonder what he meant both by "liberty" and "extremism".

Not surprisingly, around the same time the civil rights leader Martin Luther King Jr. had exactly the right corrective: "The question is not whether we will be extremists, but what kind of extremists we will be. Will we be extremists for hate or for love? Was not Jesus an extremist for love?"[15]

King Jr. provided a quote from the New Testament: *Love your enemies, bless them that curse you, do good to them that hate you, and pray for them which despitefully use you, and persecute you.*

Which camp did I call my own? Was I an evolving extremist of the Goldwater or the King Jr. variety? The truth is, I neither viewed my enemy as worthy of my blessing nor of my good will, but only of my suspicion and mistrust. I was living in the extremist world of absolutes and ultimatums. *Until this happens, then never.* In short, very Barry.

With an adolescent sense of superiority, I scolded Frank for his simplistic naïveté. It was I who believed had the inside track on how the world worked; *we* had monopoly on the truth, and until "they" came around there would never be peace.

"We are caught in an inescapable network of mutuality," King wrote, "tied in a single garment of destiny. Whatever affects us directly, affects all indirectly."[16]

I did not see it that way at the time. Frank did. He understood that there was no "us" and "them".

> ...*A word to Israel, where I real not competent. Your opinion seemed to me also a little bit one-sided. I think all communication, also in politics, is functions like a circle, there is nothing beginning and end, no cause (first cause) and effect. And it's only possible to have that pathologic circle if both sides. But today there is a false circle and everybody sees his own behaviour only as reaction to the behaviour of the others and not also a cause, reason (but it is natural). It's the same like between USA and SU, West and East. See that problem, see his own behaviour as action (cause) and reaction and is*

prepared to go a new way of thinking to beginning (like Gorbachev).

...

To his credit, Frank took me to task a bit in that letter, which was late into March. After some opening pleasantries he brought the hammer down on the nail, or on me.

I think what he was trying to say was simply this: When two parties who enter a negotiation predetermined that their side is right and the other side is wrong, and there is no middle or common ground, then finding peace is doomed from the start.

> *...Through my psychotherapy I began to think on a new way and direction in many aspects of my life and profession. So I think it is not so easy to say that only the demise of my relationship with my girlfriend has affected what I wrote in my last letter: something maybe, but there is more.*
>
> *To live with more awareness and more truth, to look at my life and my relations with more honesty. This is very difficult to explain....*

Frank's observation would come to have a profound impact on me. I wish I had taken his words to heart back then, but I was nowhere near ready for that and I had so much more to learn first. Had I been, though, I think I could have avoided quite a few missteps and wrong turns. These words and thoughts are so meaningful to me now. I didn't live by them then; I don't think I understood what they meant. I do now.

> *...Look, you wrote my life seemed rich and full (and sure it's busy and not boring) and other people think so too, but it's more outwardly seen, external. But inside of me I was not in pleasure. And I had*

> to experience that my emotional life, my inner evolution, development, grown up, my personal growth, increase stagnated and was gone not the way I wish. I have had not this kind of autonomy and I wish and need to be real free. It may look for you very abstract. A psychologist would say I'm something like neurotic. I hope you understand me right. You wrote you live life with financial restrictions. I too (I've no enough money to buy a car, which I would use very much) but money is nevertheless no problem for me today. I have enough of a good life and my real problems are from another kind, as I wrote.
>
> And that's why I like your last letter particularly, you wrote about yourself, your life, your problems, about this things which move you emotionally, inside. What do it use if we speak and wrote much about all this external things of life, about politics and business if we don't speak about this which move us on the inside. Because particularly this is important and can produce understanding of the other and real personal nearness as I wish to have with good friends.
>
> ...

The letter resumed a few days later, on April 1—what Frank called "the Foolish Day."

> ...Today is very stormy weather. I just come from the beach, with big waves and breakers. I like to walk on the beach, particularly on such weather.
>
> I find it good and interesting that you become more involved with the Jewish community. After my psychotherapy I'm for myself more interested in Jesus Christ and his history. I read again the

New Testament (the Gospel stories). Jesus Christ demonstrated for me the right practised life of LOVE in an ideal kind. The prototype of practised love in every direction. And for that love he had to die. […]
   Recently I bought a book about Jewish philosophy. I read something from Sholem Aleichem, I.B. Singer and others. Particular I like the old movement of the Chassidim the stories of Baal Shem Tov [the founder of Hasidic Judaism]. *There is a very good collection of Chassidic stories from the philosopher Martin Buber. I seldom found so much wisdom and knowledge. Recently I saw the film Yentl with and from Barbra Streisand where she visited a Talmud-school as a girl. A very good film.*
   …

Jesus Christ. Sholem Aleichem. Martin Buber. Barbra Streisand. *Quite the repertoire of knowledge and exposure for an East German!* I thought.

In 1985 Frank sent me a beautiful little book of illustrations by the great Jewish Russian artist and illustrator, Anatoli Kaplan. The book was titled *Variationen za jiddischen Volksliedern (Variations on Yiddish Folktales)*. On the title page he wrote, "For peace and friendship for my dear friend Stuart. Frank."

Frank was genuinely interested in seeking out and learning about Jewish customs and beliefs. I was deeply affected and personally overwhelmed by the gift of this book. It was the small gestures and kindnesses, and brick by brick I slowly felt the walls coming down. Not overnight. Not right away.

Frank closed this letter, returning to his search for a freedom I was myself still seeking, just in a different political time zone.

> ...Surely people need more than materialism in this vulgar kind as life is today in our consumer society. I need more.
>
> And what about GDR! Where I'm a little bit more competent. You may say the grass is greener on the other side until I get there, and later it really won't make a big difference whether I'm in the GDR and you in Canada. I understand what you mean and it's sure right for this problems—of my inside—which I occupy or deal with. On the other side there is a big difference between Canada and the GDR. You can say we are free thinking individuals with the ability to choose, and make decisions, to exercise our options, to create others. I think that is important and right; we are not children and not fools, we have all responsibility for ourselves. But sometimes I have my doubts.
>
> For me I am just dealing with this problems to find my way of living to be real free: the know the real causes of my behaviour, why I do something.
>
> I think you understand what I mean.
>
> That for today my friend. Again thanks for your letter. I am looking forward to your reply too.
>
> All my best wishes for you (for a "high awareness"!)
>
> Your friend,
> Frank

I am learning what Frank means.

In June 1989, Poland held its first free elections since 1922. Behind the Berlin Wall in 1983 I was trying to share what at the time I thought was virgin knowledge with Frank on what Solidarity was up to. He already knew!

The Solidarity trade union movement was founded in 1980 and was the first trade union not controlled by the Communist Party. Its leader was Lech Walesa. For years the government had taken harsh steps to crush the union and even imposed martial law. The movement only grew stronger and ultimately the government had no choice but to negotiate. It didn't hurt the cause either, that Pope John Paul II was Polish, born Karol Józef Wojtyła.

In December 1990, Walesa would be elected president of Poland! An unimaginable event had occurred. A pivotal point in Communism. Of course, the problem with history is that if you are living it, you have no idea how things will turn out. The truth is, history is replete with *unimaginable* events. No empire is ever so strong that it will not crumble over time. And no one is so weak or oppressed that together they cannot bring empires down. Frank ended his letter with the phrase, "for a high awareness." Words I now try to live by every day.

Saint Francis of Assisi said, "Start by doing what is necessary; then do what is possible; and suddenly you are doing the impossible."[17]

Frank comprehended that strategy intuitively. When I would dialogue about weighty global problems viewed in the grand or overarching level, he tended to frame the same problem in the language of the local, "the little man on the street", or as I like to coin it, the micro and macro of influence in our lives. And by local, I mean what was manageable and practicable. Frank was idealistic, but he witnessed how easily ideals could be turned into the instruments of oppression.

It had been five years since my last visit to Israel by the time my wife and I first visited there together. While a lot had changed in me since I left my beloved kibbutz, much more was yet to occur inside me. This trip quite literally ratcheted up the *Us vs. Them* temperature of my hardening heart, and I wasn't shy in conveying that to Frank.

> *June 11, 1989*
> *Dear Frank,*
> *I hope that all is well for you.*
> *Well, needless to say, we have returned safely from our holiday in Israel. [...] You know, a holiday in Israel is no standard holiday. [...] Israel represents something very different. It is a re-birth, a re-affirmation of a promise made over thousands of years ago. Many people have fought and died for this land (and not always over religion), and unfortunately I can tell you that many more will die in the future years. There is something very mystical in Israel. It is also a living and breathing miracle. I can't tell you properly what a thrill it was. [...] Out of nothing, the Israelis have made the desert bloom and turned the swamps into fruit-producing lands.*
> *And Frank, you must be wondering about some other aspects of Israel. The political situation, especially, in light of the "intifada". Well, firstly, this is not an intifada (uprising in Arabic). It is a war. It is a war between the two rival groups, the Arabs and the Israelis. [...]*

WHEN WALLS BECOME BRIDGES

I don't mean to try to convince you of anything. But this does come down to, what I have said before in other letters, a war.

The intifada has come down to an "US" or "THEM". Take sides if you will, object to certain tactics if you like, hope for a more fair outcome if that is possible, but understand that if you talk to me, I say that my side is right, and I understand that if you talk to the Arabs they will say that they are right.

I heard this week that two fairly important men were separately talking about bringing down the Berlin Wall...Bush and Gorbachev. Do you think that we will live to see this? I am curious, do you pass by the Wall often during your daily routine? Is there a popular jazz club that is close to the Wall? As I jog my memory, I recall that from the DDR side, one cannot get so close as one can from the West Berlin side.

Would the disappearance of the Wall cause a significant change in the life of Berliners? Would it be an opportunity that many would take as a way to go to the West? As we are about to end the decade of the eighties and look towards the nineties and the end of the twentieth century, what geopolitical changes can you see on the horizon?

For now, I must get ready for work. Keep well, and I look forward to your next letter.

Your friend,
Stuart

My next letter from Frank was indeed a surprise. Well, in hindsight, maybe not so much. He was still being the open-minded, thoughtful Frank, but in a format I was not ready for.

July 2, 1989
Dear Friend:
You may be astonished already to get a letter from me. The reason is simple. Whom shall I send this chain letter to? Although I know you are very busy I hope you will find the time for it and a friend to continue it.

I think this is not much a bad idea to support the understanding of the people from different countries. On this list will be the first from your country! I remember that you once had the idea for East–West society about a better society coming from the people sending letters to their leaders.

Nothing important news from me and my country. We have a very hot summer here.

For me I have left the "valley of sadness" and feel better now. As I said before I think this is the natural way from sadness to happiness and so forth. It is an eternal circle. If you feel all the time happy you have to ask yourself, "What is wrong?"

The policy in East Europe is more interesting than ever before. But about that more later.

You will hear from me again.
Your friend,
Frank

Frank had sent me a chain letter! The phenomenon of a chain letter first dates back to 1888 when a Methodist academy in Chicago was attempting to pay off a large amount of debt and requested that each person receiving the letter send in ten cents, and in turn mail the letter to three other unsuspecting recipients. Over the following hundred years newer and more costly variations of the chain letter appeared, and so did criminality of the practice. By the time I received Frank's chain letter I was sufficiently alert to what was wrong with it, and although Frank's chain letter was not seeking funds, just personal connections, I ignored it all the same.

Frank never wavered in his commitment to dialogue over confrontation, and in particular the dialogue versus the monologue. I was too much the podium-gripper. Even something as a benign chain letter was for Frank an opportunity to reach out over a wall to whoever might be on the other side. For Frank, meaningful change had to start at the bottom, the bottom of one's heart, and work its way up.

I am not sure I appreciated his position; however, it seemed like a good idea, but ultimately a bit naïve and impractical despite our amusing aspirations for a Nobel Peace Prize.

Frank lived in an authoritarian country, where politics was a system of a one-party rule that enforced its dictate ruthlessly from the top down, and there was no such thing as sanctioned opposition. What choice was there? Frank, I think, would have said that all systems of power—all governments, no matter how representative—are ultimately systems of coercion. As Fromm said, to have power is to exercise power.[18] To set oneself Quixote-like against that power is both difficult and futile. But Frank believed in the ultimate power of the individual to create meaningful change. After all, he was living it every day. As long as the individual has the capacity and the will to say, "No," he might say, systems of power are on notice.

It is an axiom of power that, to be effective, must be controlled. We see examples of it everyday. Why do you think a call centre puts you on hold when you have a complaint?

We play the same trick on ourselves by pretending we do not have authority over the choices we make. We put ourselves on hold. But we always have a choice. Some are too damned hard to make.

We must take responsibility for our actions and ourselves. The prominent psychotherapist and Nazi concentration camp survivor Viktor Frankl said very much the same thing. Human freedom, he wrote, was the ability and the responsibility to "choose one's attitude in a given set of circumstances."[19] Even in a concentration camp one can say, "No."

I never had an experience as profound as Frankl's—not even close. As a Jew, however, growing up in predominantly Jewish neighbourhoods, I have known numerous concentration camp survivors. Meeting so many of them personally has had a lasting impact on me. How can anyone *not* be moved by their stories and courage of survival, despite the odds against them? Some managed to adjust to a new life after the camps through the pure joy of survival and raising families out of the ashes of the Holocaust. On the other hand, far too many survivors were never able to experience any sustained joy again, and their gloomy dispositions left a lasting scar upon their children.

Frank truly believed in the power of individual personal connection, as I do today. Curtis White wrote in *The Science Delusion* that we will have had millions of missed experiences in the course of our lives that were opportunities for connections with people: on the subway, at work, at worship, at the market or out in the evening—too many to recount. I expect it is the same for most of us. We mostly sleepwalk through our days—lost for hours at a time on autopilot while we are thinking and doing—gliding along in a kind of trance.

And we have our daily problems. I wake up on the wrong side of the bed. I quarrel with a loved one. I fight with the kids. I snap at a barista who is taking too long with my latte.

Or I honk my horn impatiently at the car ahead of me. I act badly. I don't mean it.

We never do, right? Think about this: to paraphrase White, what if tomorrow you found out that every encounter you had that day—doesn't matter how big or small—would be consequential? What would happen if you treated every person you met not as a means to an end, but an end?

But that is not reality for most of us. Throughout the day we are fighting and battling for position, whether it is on the freeway with other drivers, with our partner over which cutlery to buy, or at the office with a co-worker who is criticizing our ideas. The pot is full-on boil, rarely turned down to merely a simmer.

I and *Thou*. Not *I* and *It*...

For me, *Us vs. Them* was alive and well. I was not aware of the need to change that outlook—nor was I ready to, either.

CHAPTER 8

THE BERLIN WALL FALLS

> Hope springs eternal. Unfortunately, it tends to spring prematurely.
> —Northrop Frye

September 20, 1989
Dear Frank,
I hope all is well with you.
As we were watching the TV news the other night, we saw many of your countryfolk in refugee camps in the FRG. My wife remarked, "I wonder if we'll see Frank there?"
The reports are indicating that many of these people are young, with families and that many are also professionals. Do you feel that this is accurate? I wonder if the DDR government will stop the movement of its citizens to Hungary. If not, will anyone be left in the DDR?
...

What most thought could never happen was about to happen.

Across the Communist world, old parts of a rigid political system were shaking at the core. In August, Hungary dismantled its border defences and allowed as many as 13,000 East Germans to pour across the border to freedom in Austria. And on June 4th, 1989, in Beijing, China, the Tiananmen Square massacre occurred.

The existence of the Berlin Wall, up until that time was all I had ever known. Since I was a toddler it had just been there. And I *was* there, too. It was a symbol of the once great and impregnable Soviet Empire. One expects a historic icon like that to always *be* there…but then it is not. And things are different. Like a fourteen-year-old's father, always there, never expecting anything to change until it does, and he's gone.

> *November 29, 1989*
>
> *Believe it or not, more than two months later I am finally continuing this letter. And what a two months it has been! First of all, ever since the breakthrough at the Berlin Wall, I have been trying to telephone you, which has been difficult since I don't have your phone number. I have been placing dozens of calls through the operator with the intent of getting to Berlin directly […] and hopefully to get your phone number. But no luck. So make it easy. In your next letter, please send me your phone number.*
>
> *The telephone operators told me they have never seen the telephone line circuits so busy to the DDR.*
>
> *Your letter was electrifying. I could feel the celebration; I could sense the euphoria in your voice, especially as you wrote that you now expect to travel outside of the East Bloc and hopefully one day to Canada. You would be a most welcome guest. I can remember you telling me in Berlin that perhaps at*

age seventy or eighty one would be allowed to travel to the West, and back then, in 1983, who would have speculated that your freedom would begin to arrive in 1989?

Simply amazing! Will England be your first trip?

...

I could not have been happier for Frank. What could compare to freedom? He told me once of his dream to one day visit the United Kingdom; it had seemed such folly at the time. That his dream could finally come true so quickly was beyond thinkable.

But physical freedom does not mean that one is free from our experiences of the past, as I was about to learn. Unfortunately my world, too, had been rocked by an event that in its own way was just as momentous—at least for me. My father had reappeared in my life.

> *...Maybe you don't remember what I have told you about the circumstances concerning my natural father. Okay, just a very fast history. After I turned thirteen [actually, fourteen], my parents legally separated. Before I turned fourteen [fifteen], my father left the country. He just up and abandoned a wife and two children who had no means of support. I saw him next on a visit to England and I was twenty-one. After that, I saw him here in Toronto, I was twenty-five. Last June, I bumped into him again. I am now thirty. He lives here in Toronto, by the way.*
>
> *There is a lot that happened in between all of this, none of it pleasant. My father is attempting to get back into my life and I am slowly but reluctantly allowing this to happen. My wife thinks that I'm*

crazy. I don't even dare tell my mother, she would not understand. And truthfully, I don't understand.

Do you know what drives me on this one? "Honour thy father," from the Old Testament. I have spoken to my rabbi at great lengths about this and I am still at odds with myself. Another problem is that I feel I do not need him. No, but that he needs me. He is not well, perhaps some kind of cancer though I don't think it is anything terminal. I am not willing to support him, not after all that he has done to us. What I am trying to do is to give him something, but at a very safe distance. He doesn't know anything about the baby, he has never met my wife and I am not ready to change that. I can't trust him. So, I proceed cautiously.

Well, I just wanted to tell you this. Maybe some psych therapist can help me. Do you make house calls?

...

Honour thy father (and thy mother)—there's an oldie but goodie. Number five of the Ten Commandments. Whether one is an atheist or a devout follower, most are familiar with this idiom. Clearly for me its allegiance is fraught with internal conflicts, but the notion of this implying an eternal bond; a blood bond of the highest order that has always spurred me towards some undefined earthly obligation.

For the longest time I thought his death would be a relief to me, sort of a reverse running away syndrome that would relieve me of my fear of having to deal with him or my problem with the legacy of my father any longer.

At least then the nightmare of my past would be buried once and for all. I would no longer have to fear bumping into him at a gas station, at a Blue Jays game with my wife and her family, at the hospital taking my daughter to the fracture clinic, at the local barber shop with my son…or to receive an irate phone call concerning his whereabouts. I posed a question to my rabbi at the time; we talked about my father, and I provided as many relevant details as I could recall of our checkered past.

I asked the rabbi for a *heter*, a rabbinic allowance to forgive a religious obligation, specifically of not reciting the exalted yearlong *kaddish*, the obligation of the child of a deceased parent to recite formal prayers for mourners in the daily synagogue services.

The rabbi told me unequivocally, "NO." He said that on this question, despite all that had taken place in the past, and even though he opined that I no longer had to demonstrate *kavod* (honour) on this ultimate responsibility, there would be no *heter*. For all the years prior, I had misunderstood this fundamental component of "honour thy father", the ultimate and final honour bestowed upon the dead parent by the male child.

It was for his soul that *kaddish* is recited, not for his memory or for what he did for me, although for many other mourners this *is* what they have in mind while saying *kaddish*. And on this point I felt cheated. I have attended many funerals of my friends' parents over the last number of years. When one reaches a certain age, instead of such events being a rarity, they become, unfortunately and quite naturally, a normal life cycle event. I would go to these funerals and listen to such wonderful stories of what this matriarch or patriarch did and meant to the grieving family. Anecdotes of overwhelming respect and admiration would be eulogized by children and grandchildren alike addressing the throng of visitors present, all the while choking back tears, barely able to utter those praiseworthy words of love.

I would be afforded none of that. Who would attend his funeral? What would I say? What words of comfort would I receive? What happy stories would I tell, all things being considered? My children, having not known this man personally, would only sporadically hear my less than stellar recollections of my father, and would have no reason to speak at his funeral.

For the longest time I hoped my father might return to us and that things would be different.

It was not to be. He never came back and didn't make a genuine effort to be a part of my life.

By the time I met Frank, of course, I was a grown man and had put my father and any need of him out of my mind. At least, I thought I had. In fact, in most ways imaginable my father was dead to me. Except that he wasn't.

I joked with Frank that I could use his professional help. The joke was on me. I really needed it.

When my father contacted me out of the blue (and it occurred on a couple of occasions), I quickly became very suspicious of his motives. One time in particular I would like to forget and wish it never happened. He boasted he had made a big multi-million dollar score and told me that I needed to sign some legal papers to gain my share that was to be distributed amongst his three children.

During this episode, his demeanour was unstable and explosive. I met him at his apartment to discuss this "opportunity" when he intimated that he knew some rough and unsavoury characters and wanted me to meet them. When I balked at the invitation to meet his "friends" and sign his papers he became verbally abusive. He said some unspeakably ugly things about my family and me. I became afraid of him. I waited for the least confrontational manner in which to leave, and then I did.

Just as the practically impenetrable Berlin Wall was weakening, I was surprisingly confronted by a fresh, wall-like figure of my father. It was the summer of 1989 and I was walking into a Toronto Blue Jays game. He was working as a construction security guard at the wondrous first of its kind, Toronto Skydome baseball stadium, replete with a retractable roof. It made no sense to me why he would be working security. We didn't talk much. It was very brief. The stadium had just opened and apparently he was nearing the end of his position there.

A wall is often a symbol of something gone awry.

I was clearly torn about my father and asked Frank what he thought about my responsibility to him.

So much had changed. Nothing has changed. He was my father and that is a thick bond, indeed.

> **Wednesday, January 14, 1976**
> *Dear Dad,*
> *How are you? Sorry that I didn't write you sooner, but I just got back from England.*
> *I really had a great time. Everyone was great and I saw your mother and Estelle as well. I think they would really like to hear from you, just to tell them you are OK. I hadn't been there in over three and a half years, so it was really nice seeing them all again.*

> *I sent you a long letter in September to Estelle but she couldn't forward it to you.*
>
> *I was on the school football team, the seniors team, the guys we played were all at least two years older than us. I played split end, and didn't get a pass all season.*
>
> *My writing hand is getting tired (I guess you can tell by my lazy writing). Love from your big son, Stuart. Take care.*
>
> *Stuart*
>
> *P.S. Sept. 9, I got my driver's license*

There was never anything particularly meaningful written in his replies. My father would write mostly about his big business deals he was orchestrating, including the manufacturing of hockey sticks in China. Some are made there now, in the 21st century, but in the mid-1970s not so much. Practically every letter referenced that he had completed all the work he had to so that he could come home and financially take care of his family he left back in Canada. The letters would often end with a concluding, "I will be home by such and such a time, or very soon." Looking back now, it was all so incredibly fucking surreal. Upon receiving his letters I had nothing to respond and when I did, hockey and sports was about all I could summon up the strength to comment on.

> ***Friday, March 19, 1976***
>
> *Dear Dad,*
>
> *Hi! How are you? I hope you are feeling well.*
>
> *I'm sorry I haven't written to you sooner. I even started this letter on Monday. I mean, I wrote out the envelope as soon as I got your letter and just didn't start to write.*

You didn't mention that you received the picture I sent you in my last letter. Could the government have taken it out?

I'm sending you a couple of hockey clips I hope you will enjoy. Can you get hockey news from here over there?

Today is the last day of school for a week. We get our spring break, and I could use the rest.

Take care of yourself.
All my love,
Stuart XXXX.

Thursday May 12, 1976
Dear Dad,
How are you? I'm really sorry for not writing for a while, but I've been having a few problems at school and it has been getting me down a bit. But things will work out. [The letter continues with a detailed summary of the Stanley Cup hockey series.]

The Toronto series was something else again. I don't know if you know this, but Philadelphia is the roughest team in the NHL. This series really got out of hand. The first game here I went to see it. My first ever playoff game I've ever seen. Do you remember Peter downstairs? He got tickets and he took me. I will never forget the game as long as I live.

I played golf last weekend, for my second time in two years. I have my own clubs. Remember the ones [Joe M.] gave me a few years ago? It has to be the hardest game I ever tried. And it is so frustrating.

Oh, by the way, thanks for the picture of yourself. You look great! Hey! I'm bigger than you now. I finally am getting a little broader and putting on some weight. Six feet and about 165 pounds so watch out! Everyone here is fine.

Take care of yourself. Sorry again for not writing.
All my love,
Stuart XXX

By that time he had been gone for almost a year and a half. Every letter I received was the same old bullshit. With the increased separation and slowly burning realization that he wasn't likely to come back, I started to try anything to convince him to want to come home—like seeing his son who was now bigger than him, but who was having teenage problems that require a father's guiding presence.

Sunday, May 23, 1976
Dear Dad,
How are you? We are fine. Did you hear about the Cup Finals? It's all over. Montreal won it in four straight.

[The letter goes on with more summaries of hockey and my struggles with golf.]

I'm going to end here. Oh, by the way, Frank the barber sends his regards.
Love always,
Stuart

The name of the shop was the *Playboy Barber Shop*. Of course, most of the neighbourhood boys I knew all loved getting their haircut there because the shop owner stocked *Playboy* magazines. And that was a pretty big deal back then because it was the only way we could see naked women—except in *National Geographic*, which wasn't nearly as much fun. The magazines were kept under the cash register stand and we were allowed to take one as long as we didn't make a nuisance. The one rule was to make sure they were returned as they were found and didn't leave them out on the table in the waiting area. I was okay with that—we all were—but years later I couldn't help but wonder what they were hiding from. (It wasn't like the name *Playboy Barber Shop* was fooling anyone.)

The letters I received from my father were all the same. He did not respond to my attempted calls for help when I was feeling down; he wrote about his big deals and him coming home. I felt alone.

> **Thursday, September 30, 1976**
> Dear Dad,
> HI. How are you? I'm really very sorry for not writing you for so long. I can't remember if I even thanked you for the birthday card you sent me. If not, thank you.
> I had an extremely tiring and hard summer. After school let out late in June I started summer school. I didn't do too well last year so I decided if I took two subjects in summer school it would be easier this year. It was very hard, but I didn't do too bad.
> The day school finished I went down to the Ex and started my job down there on the midway. I worked for twelve to sixteen hours a day for seventeen straight days. The day the Ex finished the next day school started again.
> Lately I have been feeling down about personal problems. You know those "adolescence blues"? But I will pull through just like every other teenager.
> I think I'm still growing. I'm pretty close to six-foot-one but I'm not quite there yet. I'd like to go over 170 pounds.
> Take care, Dad. I'm really sorry about not writing.

I love you,
Stuart XXX

I made yet another special declaration to my father about my size. It was important to me for him to know that I was bigger than he was—though what I meant by this was unclear. Was my meaning literal only or metaphorical? This was the last I heard from him for several years. Even his family in England told me he had just disappeared, not to be heard from for over two years.

I used to think I saw my father when I was out. It transformed into a fear that I would randomly see him again—and not be ready for it. I think having a sense of being "ready" was something I always needed. His face would appear ghosted in a shop window or as someone in a crowd or just walking along the street. This continued even after his funeral. It scared the hell out of me. Why did this happen? Once I startlingly saw his face in mine after a squash match at a friend's apartment. I was sitting on the floor exhausted, opposite a squared pillared mirror wall when I looked up and thought I was him.

I tried so hard in these letters to maintain an upbeat and confident tone with him, but I also felt conflicted and disloyal to my mother. I tried to be matter-of-fact and casual. Like, no big deal, Dad. You're gone but we can still be pals. Of course, I was dying inside. How could he have just up and left us? How could he have promised he was coming back when he knew he wouldn't be? How could he not send any money to Mom?

Nothing but questions. Never any answers. After a while, it just seemed pointless. I blocked it all out. I thought I was numb to it.

I received my next letter from Frank on December 26. How exciting it was to find mail waiting for me from Berlin—now the city without a wall.

> Dear Stuart,
>
> For Christmas I come to the lake, but I want to wish you a Happy New Year. I hope you have had more nice and calm days on the end of 1989, which real was very turbulent and exciting. May be more for us than for you. The Brandenburg Gate is open. From GDR to FRG and also from FRG to GDR people don't need a visa! You cross the border without any problems. At New Year's I will have a party with friends in West Berlin. This is the new way of life here.
>
> But of course this euphoria don't last too long. People can't live very long from this new feeling of freedom and then all the old personal problems come again on the surface. And on the other side it becomes more difficult how to give democracy here in GDR our own face, this is not too simple, but people are engaged to do that. A lot of parties [political] are founded from the left, to more right, the whole spectrum. And the electioneering has already began. First free elections will be on 6 May. I still don't know which party I will give my vote.
>
> I'm more for basic democratic work as the New Forum has done. But I fear they want to become a party too, to which we have enough now. I think chances for the new reformed communist government are not so bad.
>
> A lot of people and especially the West (FRG) politics speak about reunification of Germany. I think it shall and will have to come but the question

is, when? And on which way. I wouldn't like it if the reunion comes now together with a national feeling. I think we should take us time for this process to go step by step as it is (my opinion) necessary we here in GDR develop our own—may be socialist—democratic system which is in good function, at first to have to learn to live with and in democracy. And then a reunion is possible together in a whole European union process. On this way it is possible we can give the democratic movement some new ideas, why not?

On the other side there are the economic problems and the economical situation in GDR is not so good, more bad and need the cooperation with the West economy.

Among the left intelligence they say we shall go—try it—our own way of real socialist democracy—not simple a copy of the West society—the consumer society. But a lot of the people have not the patience for that. They want the reunion because they hope to get on this way quickly the same high living standard as in FRG (the best would be without the work).

But the international political situation is not so that a reunion is possible and so we have still some years time. Especially the NATO-Warsaw Pact problem hinders this, and the other European countries and Israel are also not too happy about the fact in particular, because the right national forces come more and more ahead. This is a real danger I see too.

The socialist world system is dead!

It was a real chain-reaction. Last not least, Rumania, and most terrible. I was three weeks there *and know the situation there very good from some visits, particularly through my German friends there which live in a village near Timisoara, the centre of the resistance. Life is so very hard and poor there and they may need help more than any other. Question is which parts of the socialist ideal can still be alive? Or nothing? 1990 will become a very interesting year. I don't know enough about economical mechanisms and what is needed here to work more effectively. I think it would not be hard to try some alternative ideas but I fear people have not enough patience for such experiments.*

Erich Fromm said that a society and economy which is in its function depending from a higher and higher level of consumption is not the right way. We should think of that today and here if we think about alternatives.

About my personal life is not much to say. In the meantime, I changed the hospital and now I'm working on the university hospital of Berlin where I've studied before. I don't like such big and impersonal conditions but for the next two years it's necessary for my education.

And sorry still nothing new in love. Only this or another relation but not that is right for me. Sure this is no accident. Nothing is accidental in these things. I'm still not ready. There are some reasons and I know it will change.

This is for today my friend. 1990 you will hear from me again. I wish you all the best for the New Year.

Your friend,
Frank

As was mentioned earlier, Erich Fromm was another powerful influence on Frank's outlook. Fromm had an interesting insight on where communism had gone wrong, insights with which I think Frank would wholeheartedly agree: "It succumbed to the spirit of capitalism which it had wanted to replace. Instead of understanding it as a movement for the *'liberation of man',* communism was incorrectly seen 'as being exclusively a movement for the economic improvement of the working class.'"[20] Instead of transcending a system, socialism became a movement for the disadvantaged and exploited to take their place *in the system.*

Often in his letters following the fall of the Wall he would mention that despite the freedom now realized that so many had longed for, people felt widespread anxiety at how rapidly the old system had yielded to the new, and questioned whether the benefits were all to be admired. "When man is transformed into a thing," Fromm wrote, "and managed like a thing, his managers themselves become things; and things have no will, no vision, no plan. With the bureaucratic management of people, the democratic process becomes transformed into *a ritual.*"[21]

The idea that we can become unthinking cogs in a ritual under the pretence of freedom would come to have profound meaning for me in my own struggles with my faith and who I was.

Fromm wrote: *"If a man can only obey and not disobey, he is a slave; if he can only disobey and not obey, he is a rebel (not a revolutionary); he acts out of anger, disappointment, resentment, yet not in the name of a conviction or a principle."* [22]

What did I really discern versus what had I become merely comfortable with or complacent about? I had surely become complacent about my father and his ongoing subliminal impact on my life. Yet I naïvely dismissed the notion that I had "baggage" from my past.

Frank was struggling with his newborn freedom and also fighting his own complacency with such fast-paced change and in doing so, was discovering his true understanding of *freedom*. I was not ready for that in my life; in fact, I was going in the opposite direction.

> *February 1, 1990*
> Dear Stuart,
> Hello my friend! No more "behind the Iron Curtain"!
> The best greetings I send to you with this letter from the new year.
> How can I tell you how the situation is here? All things are going faster and faster than anyone can think. No one gives a prognosis. The electioneering is in full speed and all are awaiting the election results of May. Time will certainly bring important new developments. We have about twenty different parties here from the left and the right. All speak for reunion so fast as possible (except of the very left-wing parties) to have social market economy, and a European house, freedom and peace, and so on. All the same, not very different.
> Every weekend you can find here Kohl, Gorbachev and a lot of other VIP of the FRG policy (VIP = very important person).
> The hate of the people is so big, their anger, rage about all what is happening in the last forty years under the name socialism. They say: we could be so big and rich as in FRG but now after this experiment

we are poor. The cities and the nature are dirty and destroyed, our industries is a bitter ruin, nothing productivity. Nobody asks for ideals. They look for the facts and on this point you find mainly chaos, economy about to collapse.

...

Frank had freedom, but with newfound awareness unearthed fresh problems as he saw himself being transformed by freedom into Fromm's *thing* (cog). He also addressed my delicate problem.

The letter breaks off and resumes a few days later.

...Life here is more interesting than ever before. It is not easy but I am happy about all the new possibilities.

All people call: we are the victims and forget: we are all guilty, we were, are—forever—the culprit and the victims. We should never forget this fact, if we want to understand how it could happen, to stay also in humbleness. If we don't see our guilt—and this is the big danger—we will make again the same mistakes. After dictators of Stalinism will follow the dictators of the market and money (sure it's a thousand times better than Stalinism) but I think it's also not the big happiness and after all, for our souls, is the difference so big? My leading word: the way is all, the aim is nothing.

You were frightened about the development in USSR. And that's right. I am too. But you see Gorbachev understands the signs of the new time. Now they will give up his power monopoly and come also to a parliamentary democracy. I think that is the right way.

> *What shall I say about your father? I can understand your interest in him. He is simply your father and you are a part of him. On the other side: you real don't need him. (And I think you are not real responsible for him.) If you want to let take part him on your life and give him something—at very safe distance—it can be o.k. But you have to ask yourself why you are want to do it, what are your expectations to him... You should know that, then it can be alright. You should speak with him about your expectations and wishes and his or you relations. May be that you can find then a practicable way of handling the situation.*
>
> *And of course good luck and happiness with your child! As sure,*
> *Your friend,*
> *Frank*

They say that there are no coincidences. It was ironic that both Frank and I were confronted by profound circumstances in life at the same time. Frank was now free due to the fact that the shackle of the Warsaw Pact alliance astonishingly and swiftly became a relic of history but we were still both hampered by our respective pasts.

> **February 12, 1990**
> Dear Frank,
> As they say over here, "the times they keep a-changing"! It is becoming hard to keep up with all that is going on in the world. At least my little piece of it. My wife is about to begin her final three months of the pregnancy and that only thing that will "keep changing" will be diapers. [...]

> *I should go back and take some more political science classes because my predictions are not working out too well. Instead of calling my thoughts predictions, I should just call them preferences. As of today, it certainly looks as though there will again be one Germany sometime in the near future. As you can imagine that bothers me, concerns me. I can fully understand the rationalistic aspirations that Germans would have. That is perfectly logical. But I am concerned about the neo-Nazi right wing and they do have a political constituency particularly in West Germany. It will be the task of your leaders to keep a watch on the Right.*
>
> ...

Was Frank's freedom worth the risk of a re-galvanization of fascist elements in a unified German society? Was the muffled sound of a wall to be replaced with the returning clamour of soldiers' goose steps under the Brandenburg Gate? Was the peace and serenity with the absence of my father worth the potential storm by accepting him back into my life? They say that eighty to ninety percent or more of what we fear never materializes.

> **June 24, 1990**
> Dear Frank,
> Yesterday I celebrated my thirty-first birthday and for the first time I received a birthday card from a new source…my first child! Now I can say with delight, hope, and optimism that my life, our lives, will never be the same again.
> Yesterday on television I saw Checkpoint Charlie being dismantled. Certainly I have memories of passing through this infamous and iconic bit of

history. But, more so, I feel despair that it was ever erected. How long was it there? Twenty-eight? Twenty-nine years? How many unfortunate people were killed because of it and the Wall, and for what?

I remember when you and I met and we were discussing the realities of your situation. You told me you didn't think you would ever travel outside of the Eastern Bloc countries. Oh, you did concede that it might happen on your eightieth birthday.

And here you are, a young man with a more extensive education that myself (a doctor no less!), clearly a very intelligent and articulate man, who only seven years ago had no hope of achieving his dreams. The political circumstances of seven years ago led you and millions of others to believe that nothing would ever change, at least not in your lifetime. But the winds of change did come and apparently they came so easily. We were all caught off guard; we didn't expect it. We didn't see it coming. But it happened.

And I am thrilled for you. But what a waste. What a terrible waste.

Best wishes!

Stuart

P.S. Well, as you can see it took quite some time to finish this letter. Did you celebrate the World Cup victory by West Germany?

What a waste, indeed. There was the Berlin Wall and then it was torn down. My father was there and then he was gone. Opposite realities of waste, lost opportunities and fractured lives—time that could never be replaced. We can't turn back the clock and pretend none of it ever happened.

Subconsciously and by no coincidence Frank and I found comfort from one another at pivotal times in our lives. He was the only one I could reach out to without shame or judgment, and share in a way that was foreign to me and maybe foreign to many men of the time. Who knew it would take a wall to draw me to a central force in my life in June of 1983? The same wall would bring us consolation and unity when it no longer stood in 1990.

CHAPTER 9

THE BOIL

The way to see by faith is to shut the eye of reason.
—Benjamin Franklin

January 1994
Hello my dear and true friend Stuart!
What a surprise, as I got your small parcel with the T-shirt and your letter. I enjoy very much that our contact didn't broke.
A lot is happened since you've heard last time from me. On the photographs you see me and my girlfriend in Rome. We are together now about nearly two years and think about that she comes with her things in my flat. Her name is Katharina and she just finished her study in psychology and she is looking now for a good job. [Discusses how he passed his exams but was laid off from his job. Applied for a new job at a clinic for psychosomatics, which he got. He talks about being very busy.]

The "new times" are very straining. "Money makes the world go around" as it says.

As I see from your letter a lot is changed in your life too. You got your second child, changed your flat, a new job and so your responsibility increase. Meanwhile I can imagine too to have children and it will depend how the relation to Kathy will develop.

The life in the unified Germany after four years become more and more "normal," in particular as well as we still have two Germanies. The real reunion needs much more time and thought. On the surface people are able to adapt to the new and often opposite demands and they try it very much and often sorry without thinking about that, about the process of changing. It looks like someone put on the new and better seeming... [rest of letter very unclear].

How do you think about the approximation of Israel and Palestinian and Syria? I think it is not the baddest way but as I know you, you are not in pleasure with the process. But I fear more for Russia and the impossible way to democracy and for the psychopathic Vladimir Zhirinovsky.

Excuse me for the hectical finish of the letter but I'm under pressure. This is the first letter I wrote for anyone for months! You will hear from me again.

Your friend,
Frank

When the one prince of our family arrived, I was so proud to have a son. I still am. I remember fondly how precious that that little boy was. So many wonderful memories now. It's hard to believe that little boy is now a man.

Frank talked about Germany after four years returning to the "normal" of a unified Germany. Of course, the quotation marks he used suggested the opposite. Like, who the hell knows what normal is, anyway.

I think of my own life, and I'm not sure what was happening. I was spending more and more time immersed in my faith. To an orthodox Jew, that can mean checking your life of freedom at the door and taking on a regimen of the three "Rs": *rules, regulations and rituals*—that quite literally order your day from sunup to sundown, seven days a week. Even if one needs to relieve oneself during the night, there are rules to be followed, as well!

There is a story about the Jews, God and the Old Testament (Torah). Before the Jews became the "chosen people", God offered the Torah to the other nations of the world first—one by one—but He was turned down by all of them until the only people left to consider the offer were the Jews who were camped at the foot of Mount Sinai.

"Seriously, these are a lot of commandments."

"Six hundred and thirteen, to be exact." Not only the ten!

"That seems like a lot."

The Jews dithered in their response.

God then wrapped his arms around Mount Sinai and wrestled it up from the earth and hung it menacingly over the Jews, all standing literally underneath the mountain.

"Are you sure you don't want my Torah?" Although conveyed in jovial fashion, this story has Talmudic origins. The

Jews accepted the Torah and thereafter became the "chosen people". Perhaps *"chosen"* by default.

There were several motives that comfortably guided me into the orthodox lifestyle. Even so, it took quite a number of years until my family and I fully embraced it and many of the accompanying rituals.

One was my deep and passionate affection for Israel and I loved being amongst people who shared that common thirst. It fulfilled a potent emotional need I had to belong and to feel accepted. The rituals and commandments were not a burden to me, at least not at first. I loved pretty much everything about them. Living a heavily ritualized religious life actually grounded me and brought contentment.

When I first came back to Canada from my overseas trip at the end of 1983 I began attending synagogue, although it was not entirely with a religious purpose in mind; it was nationalistic and linguistic. I had every intention of moving to Israel in the not-too-distant future, and being in synagogue was my unorthodox and illogical way of keeping up my conversational modern Hebrew. After all, there is not much Hebrew of any kind spoken in the streets of Canada, nor is there much Aramaic or biblical Hebrew (the language of the prayer books) spoken in the streets of Israel, but I felt I kind of killed two birds with one stone. In time, the spiritual benefits of regular synagogue attendance unquestionably emerged and marginally sustained the Hebrew I learned in Israel.

Throughout my life I found it difficult to really feel understood by anyone, and perhaps surprisingly (even shockingly to many), inside I lived a lonely, disconnected existence. Within the modern orthodox community, however, I found myself very much at ease with what appeared to me as this great monolithic melting pot where deeply felt values were commonly shared and openly discussed. In addition, I felt, as did many others leading the nearly identical lifestyle, that we were doing something everlasting for our faith, our children and our children's children by encasing ourselves in the comfort and protection of the Torah and the Torah lifestyle. The future of the Jewish people was secured by our life choice—or so I yearned. The worry about my earthly pursuits and ultimate destiny also helped propel me into the welcoming distractions and eternal application of orthodoxy. There I found common communal goals, ideals and also an unparalleled mutual support network. The community warmly sustained one another equally during celebratory times and times of struggles.

Reminders often surfaced that I had not completely abandoned my secular past and the vestiges of a non-religious lifestyle. A letter from Frank was the primary anchor to the person I was still searching to discover and liberate. To this day, few cause me to think and to contemplate as does he.

> **September 1994**
> *Hallo Stuart, my friend and how are you?*
> *As you ask me, I am well at most of the time, and sometimes not, as you see with me and here it's like everywhere—no surprise. But a real surprise was your letter with which I didn't count so soon.*
> *I just sit here with a Georgian tea and "Long Wood," as you sure know a Canadian pure malt whisky. Since I was in Scotland I like to drink whisky. Kati is outdoor with a friend in a pub, it is a girlfriend of my friend and it seems they need to complain to one to the other over their impossible men and speak about endless difficulties of relationship. And after our holiday we have much more difficulties than*

good days, sorry, but I hope for better days. […] It may sound strange for you, for a people who live in religion, belief and with God. I sometimes ask me how it would be to be in such situation, which give you orientation, show you the right direction to go and live, may be the continuation of the way your grandfathers and more back. I got the impression that you stay steady in your family and in your origin. Sometimes I feel envious of you or of people which have such deep sure ground to stay in, such meaning given orientation in their live. That's it, what I search for with the help of psychotherapy for the last five years. I'm grown up without any kind of belief, of religion—the communist ideology, the Marxism-Leninism really couldn't take this function—and ever ask me what is the meaning of life.

I remember in school it was once the theme of a paper and I wrote the meaning of life is to search for the meaning. It was of course not the Marxist answer of this question and I got a bad mark from my, as I thought, intelligent paper. In fact it was far away from the knowledge about this problem. Now I feel more near the answer, theoretically but the realization in practise seems me more difficult as ever before. And this moment I meet you again what you have written in your letter about your problems of how to earn enough money. This problem bind up us very close and fixed: "Money make the world go around." In the "new times" after 1989 I have had to understand it. The dictatorship of the money sometimes is much more harder than the dictatorship of the "proletariat" as we have had it before.

> *Today I would recommend you watch your children for one day and you will understand what the meaning of life is—or look for a cat... We just got one "instead of" a child, a male, now ten weeks old. We call him Willy.*
>
> *...*

I still laugh at the cat joke.

Perhaps Frank's school paper was subliminally influenced by Frankl's *Man's Search For Meaning*. Frankl wrote, "Man's search for meaning is the primary motivation in his life and not a 'secondary rationalization' of instinctual drives."[23] It took a while for me to become consciously aware of that.

It should be clear by now that Frank was as bad as I was when it came to mailing his letters. The following is the second half of the letter he composed in September, but did not get around to dropping in the mail until two months later.

> *...November and you can grumble—but that is my situation, the weeks are gone over, filled with a lot of work and I didn't found the time to continue the letter and sometimes I forget that "we don't live to work but work to live" and forget that it should bring a little fun.*
>
> *We [Kati and Frank] are together now nearly three years. Since March we live together, she moves into my flat which was the larger one. Kati like to wear your T-shirt from the ice hockey team as night-clothes.*
>
> *A year ago she finished her study as a psychologist and now she has a job on the university to write her promotion about the changing identity of the people of the east and the west after 1989. She is very nice.*

> *She is 26. She is enough hysterical and sometimes really not easy to take and I could account still a lot of more "good and bad" attributes but not to forget the most important: I love her.*
>
> *Recently Arafat and Rabin got the peace-Nobel-prize. I fear you are not so pleased with this fact, isn't it?*
>
> *…*

To his credit, Frank correctly intuited that I responded to the awarding of the Nobel Peace Prize to Yasser Arafat as a cruel hoax. It was, of course, a fantastically controversial decision by the Norwegians to jointly award the peace prize to Arafat and Israeli Prime Minister Yitzhak Rabin for their work on the Oslo Accords and the Arab-Israeli peace process. As *Time* magazine said in its banner headline, "One man's terrorist is another man's freedom fighter."

Oddly, this reminded me of a brief relationship I had in 1980.

I was home for the summer from university after a difficult year of studies. I had decided to switch out of my declared program of Public Administration and into a more general combined major of Economics and Political Science. The upshot was that I would not be completing my three-year degree in three years. I could have taken summer classes to build up credits but I was looking forward to a summer of what I hoped would be bacchanalian hedonism. Well, one night a bunch of us headed to the beer garden at the famed Ex in Toronto to test the limits of our imagined debauchery.

I was never a Don Juan, but like most young men with several pints of courage under their belt I suddenly felt irresistible and somehow I met a gorgeous young blonde woman who seemed enchanted by me and my sparkling wit. I could not help noticing that every time I said anything she would sparkle dreamily and stare at me in adoring, smiling silence. I finally realized my error of perception: she spoke very little English. Well, no matter! This was a pure animalistic, physical attraction. It turned out she was an au pair from Germany. Clearly my anti-German deportment did not apply to beautiful German women who happened to be interested in me.

We started hanging out together. One night back at my apartment (my brother and I at this point were living in a small unit in the same building as Mom and Gil—paid for by Gil!) we were lounging on the chesterfield (a result of my Anglophile disposition on using British expressions whenever I could). The *telly*—had been turned on as background distraction. I must have had it tuned to a news program because just as we sat down, an image of then Israeli Prime Minister Menachem Begin came on, and she quite surprisingly and suddenly sneered and rolled her eyes towards the TV. As for Begin himself, when commander of the Irgun, many would say he was a terrorist fighting the British prior to Israeli independence in 1948.

Her guttural revulsion at the sight of Begin stopped me in my tracks.

Was her reaction political or racial? Did she know I was Jewish? I should have asked, but I was preoccupied with more pressing short-term goals.

A few days later I was invited to a family friend's cottage for the day and took my German date along. These friends were Jewish, as were nearly all my friends growing up. I never gave a second thought to her presence being an issue. But it was.

The second my friends heard her German accent the walls went up. Suddenly the atmosphere transformed.

Though they were perfectly polite and reserved at what they had realized, it was me they later and privately voiced their displeasure to. This family was not religious in the slightest. They traditionally celebrated the main Jewish holidays at home by regularly hosting a lovely annual Passover Seder and Rosh Hashana dinner to which my family were routinely invited. They were very upset with me by my German guest's presence.

"What are you thinking? What are you up to bringing someone like her here? This isn't something serious, is it?" In no uncertain terms, they let it be known that I had leapt a boundary and had committed an act of tribal treason. I felt like a collaborator who was being shamed for my despicable duplicity of sleeping with the enemy.

I was stunned. Genealogically, they were a Jewish Canadian family going back a few generations. *Surely they must have met many German Canadians*, I thought. *They can't still be fighting the Nazis in 1980 in cottage country?*

On the other hand, my girlfriend could have been anti-Semitic. At least in retrospect, I think she was. How else to explain her disgust solely with an image of Begin? It is unlikely she merely didn't appreciate what he said. After all, her English was poor and her Hebrew even worse! I have noticed a similar reaction with certain opponents to former American President Barack Obama. It isn't anything overt or obvious. It's a lot more subtle. The criticism levelled at him seems a bit more passionate than it would be were he Caucasian.

A *"them"* always needs an *"us"* and vice versa.

Freedom fighter or terrorist? Lovely young German woman or spawn of Hitler? And the answer is, of course, that it all depends on which side of the fence (or wall) you're on.

In my letter I resolutely supported the side with those who said Arafat was an "unrepentant terrorist with a long legacy of promoting violence" for terrorist campaigns against Israel.[24] Of course Arafat had his supporters; I was definitely not among them. Once again, however, Frank had taken the long view and saw the award as a positive step.

> ...But after all, I think it is not the best solution and the necessary step in the right direction. The future will show it, but who thought that the peace between Israel and Egypt would bring so good results. And now the Palestinian people have to do with themselves. The fight between PLO and Hamas is not decided and will not be solved so fast.
>
> ...

Frank was certainly right about that last point. It is interesting to me today as I sense the contrasting tones between his letters and mine. What an intriguing irony, after all, that Frank had been born and grew up in an authoritarian country where liberties were severely limited, and yet he consistently resisted anything in speech or habit or belief that was rigidly doctrinaire; I, on the other hand, enjoyed all the freedoms he lacked, but I increasingly adopted the authoritarian tone.

What I admire so much about Frank is how he seeks out alternatives to what might be a more characteristically knee-jerk reactionary and dogmatic approach. He has that refreshing Spinozan passion for the good and the true and the beautiful—whatever that might be, and wherever it might be found. What I have noticed about open-minded people in my life is how unassuming and generous they are.

Frank and I finally started to lay the groundwork to bring us together again since that fateful day in East Berlin so many years before. I longed to share personal time again with my most nonpartisan companion.

> ...I found it very nice idea to invite us to Canada. Sure once we will come to your home, also in case we couldn't say it today when. Did I tell you that I have already long a particular affinity to the Jewish culture. In Berlin after the 1989 the Jewish parish growth a little bit up, at most Russian Jews and particular the Jewish cultural sense became very active and interesting. Every year here take place a great Jewish cultural festival and we visited the concerts of such fine Klezmatic-groups like the "Klezmatics" and "Brave old World." In East Berlin is found a good theater and was built up a Jewish Center just beside the renovated old synagogue in Oranienburger street (which was formerly the biggest synagogue of Berlin but now is not used for God- service.)
>
> So it remain for me to wish you and your family a Happy New Year and particular some fine and quiet days at the end of 1994. You will hear from me again. All the best.
> Your friend,
> Frank

While Frank had a certain preconceived notion of what my religious life might look like when he would eventually arrive in Canada to see me, I was preparing to enter the lifestyle in ways he could not have possibly imagined.

In 1995 we took the final plunge and commitment to Orthodox Judaism, modern orthodoxy, that is. We accepted mostly the same religious stringencies, but chose to live in and embrace the modern contemporary world. As an example for men, our apparel and appearance was conventional and would not typically include the long black jackets, fedoras, beards or sidelocks that are commonly associated with ultra- or Haredi Orthodox men.

There was nothing casual about the lifestyle, however. In my experience it was less a lifestyle than a life sentence at a maximum security prison. Actually, even in maximum security there are TV privileges, though we did not go so far as to ban TV from our home as some others do. Rules governed our behaviour from the moment we woke up until we went to sleep. We voluntarily submitted ourselves to a yoke that controlled, directed, and regulated virtually, as Sting and The Police sing, "…every breath you take, every move you make [and] every bond you break." It told us how and with whom to socialize, where we could eat, what we could eat and how our food could be prepared. Our rituals guided us on how our children would be named, how we would be married (and divorced), how our bodies would be prepared for burial after we died, and how we would grieve; our rituals specified precisely how we prayed, where we prayed and how often and if God was listening, how we celebrated religious holidays and how and what we blessed upon eating and gazing on particular sites and some very particular laws to be followed on family purity. For me there was virtually no aspect of living, personal or communal, that was not overshadowed by some custom, habit, rule, prohibition or observance. The word *Torah,* after all, means "instructions for living." It therefore stands to reason that a Torah-observant individual will follow the Torah to guide them in life—ALL aspects of life.

Despite all this I found the lifestyle, at least in my formative years of observance, immensely liberating, fulfilling and rewarding—and no doubt so do the multitude that follow this lifestyle and its obligations. The more I gave myself over to my new-way-of-life template, the more I felt free of extraneous demands and anxieties that had plagued me for so long. The never-ending cares and concerns that wore me down in my "secular" life was met with relief in the religious life. The Sabbath (Shabbat) was a treasured time, and the communal social dynamics of Shabbat and religious holidays (especially in one of those tightly configured Jewish neighbourhoods) were particularly settling.

Rabbi Sacks wrote of being a young student who was instructed that the "law was the lifeblood, the DNA, of Judaism, and it was more than the mere regulation of conduct. It was a way of being in the world."[25]

I felt for the first time in my life that I was *in the world*—it was a relevance that mattered greatly to me. I felt I truly belonged. I felt closer to my wife and united as a couple; having a resolute lifestyle to share together and raising children in that environment simply felt like the right way of being in the world—all of us together.

Our extended family, however, felt we had gone mad or worse—that we had been brainwashed and joined a cult. Actually, my wife's family was a bit more accepting with our decision than my family was, but not by much. I had a particularly hard time with my stepfather, Gil. He rarely showed us respect for our decision. In fact, he was often condescending and dismissive. "What is the point of living a nonsensical religious life here in Canada?"

He made it clear through his unsolicited opinion that we had made a "stupid" decision. It made no difference to him that he had never lived a religious life and that we made the choice to live that way—or that we had lived a secular lifestyle—and it didn't seem to matter to him that we might be more informed than he was when it came to the comparative choice we made.

We would try to explain several times over. "We know exactly what secular life is like," we would say. "We grew up secular. However, we have explored the deeply religious life, and we actually prefer it to the secular. We know both. You know only one. So who are you to judge?"

Some people understood, or at least eventually they stopped trying to argue us out of the decision we had taken and I guess that isn't the same as accepting it or being happy about it or our choices we freely made. Interestingly, it was Frank who stood out of all the friends I knew who expressed no judgment one way or another, and only tried to envision the richness of our decision.

I had absolutely no doubts about my commitment. None. I loved the community, the bonds, the rituals and the powerful sense of identity it created for me. I enjoyed the regularity it imposed on my life, like the structure around prayer times, weekdays, as well as on the Shabbat. I felt faithfully centred and purposeful for the first time in my life. The cynic will easily dismiss these features as symptoms of a deep need on my part for regulation and order.

Well, a deep need is still a need and it often doesn't matter what the answer is, as long as it addresses the need. Did orthodoxy immunize me from a malaise of *outsiderness?* It did.

The composer Gustav Mahler said that he was three times an exile. "I am three times without a homeland."[26] As a Bohemian in Austria, an Austrian among Germans and as a Jew throughout the world—always an intruder, never fully welcomed.

Growing up in Toronto, Canada; born in the UK; surprised as a child upon discovering myself to be Jewish; always with a confused identity, I felt welcome in the modern orthodox community. I no longer felt like a wanderer. I thought, too, that this new lifestyle was helping to make me a better person. And that it would help make me a better husband and father. I also felt that I (we) were expanding the base of the Jewish people of the world by spawning little clones of ourselves… and wasn't that a wonderful thing to do?

From the moment I met Frank behind the Berlin Wall, there was something instantly familiar and comfortable about him. We are but six months apart in age. Physically, Frank and I are just about the same height and slender body type—then and now.

On that late spring day in East Berlin, Frank was wearing a brown corduroy blazer, a light yellow and beige plaid shirt and faded blue jeans with a satchel over his shoulder, as was his student colleague who was with him. His voice was assertive and confident, but with no arrogance.

Astonishingly, his complexion was rather pale for a warmer time of the year, probably on account of all the time he spent studying indoors; however, the most distinguishing mental image I have of Frank was his haircut. One might think he used a bowl over his head to cut his own hair, but a jagged one, as his bangs were terribly uneven. *So communist,* I (embarrassingly) remember thinking. When Frank spoke, however, there was nothing uneven or jagged about him. He most definitely thought before he uttered his words, partly due to him being customarily guarded at first to Western strangers as he would later tell me, but he was also trying to be as articulate and as clear as possible.

His heavily German-accented English was a struggle for him, but he made himself perfectly understandable to myself and my two American companions. Even then as a medical school student, he came across as erudite beyond his years and in a strange sense, worldly despite locked behind an Iron Curtain of repression and limited personal freedoms. He was, in a stereotypical sense, a contradiction.

At the end of our day in East Berlin we all exchanged addresses, but to my knowledge, after that day only Frank and I communicated with one another.

Needless to say, the trust and openness that was evident from day one between Frank and I blossomed over the years. It is hard to imagine what life would be like or how it would have evolved without our friendship. There are few people on life's journey who make a profound impact on that life. We are moulded by our parents, shaped by our children and our romantic partner, but the gratitude and indebtedness I hold for a precious few souls not related to me is immeasurable. Frank is one of them.

> *January 1996*
> Dear Stuart,
> *Thank you for your open-hearted and as ever very amuse letter.*

Recently we saw again Woody Allen's film—I don't know the original title (translated "The City Neurotics"). It's the film where he says at the beginning, he would never join a club which accept him as a member. I really love him and his kind of humor. I remember that because in the film he always speaks over his therapist.

I just listen to Tim Buckley, which is really fine music, do you know him? Because he is mostly forgotten. I discovered him a year ago. He was one of the extraordinary artists of the flower-power or hippie-time in the United States (he lived in Venice, California) and he took the same fate as others of the famous musicians like Jim Morrison (his Doors I like particular) or Jimmy Hendrix. With collecting CDs I spend much marks, as you know Jazz is one of my obsessions. I still play self saxophone for six years and recently we have had a little concert on a congress of our psychotherapy institute with a new founded little quartet with piano, trumpet, drums and my saxophone.

The second part. *I feel very well...* [Frank explains a back problem he mentioned in the first part of this letter is clearing up] *...and I hope you are so well.* [Talks about job change.] *Now I work on a so called "closed" ward for acute psychiatric cases as the different forms of psychosis or for suicidal patients. It is very interesting and very different to my former work. And it's a really necessary experience for a man who want to work as a psychotherapist. It is important to see and to get to know how to handle or to treat people with such a deep and severe psychical pathology. I don't know if you ever* *had contact with a psychotic men. But sure you can imagine that it is really difficult to feel in their kind of seeing, experience, feeling and it is important for me to understand. [...]*

You get a third child! Our best wishes you are very brave, what shall we say? Kati and I, we live now together for four years and I become older and older, meanwhile I am 36. I think we shouldn't wait much longer. She is 27 and in no hurry. We will see but I would like. Really we sometimes spoke about visit you in Canada this summer. In the case you get your third child in July we better have to wait for a year, because you will have than other responsibilities as to be with us.

Congratulations for your one more career step up. In fact, it's not necessary to tell me that the live is expensive today, especially with children. It's the same here. The life here is really not becoming cheaper for the last years, in the opposite. Sure you have listen about the social crisis in Germany with around 11 percent unemployment (more than 4 million people), the highest rate since world war two, the increase of taxes and what you have to pay for security (particular pension and health) and the decrease rates for unemployment and the rent for our flat is almost again increased. But don't be in anger, we live well. I want only to tell that meanwhile six years after 89 for me the west is normal and nevertheless the people in the East are still the same, are still from the East and the they from the West are the same as before.

The identity of the people are deeper and stronger as someone may have thought. Particular

> *before 89 we lived more quiet, with more calm, you could say we lived more slowly. In the last few years for me became the term "slowlieness" more and more central.*
>
> *...*

Frank was referencing *Slowness,* a novel by the Czech writer Milan Kundera. Kundera was unhappy with the pace of life created by modern technology. His point was that the modern obsession with speed and efficiency was destroying opportunities for intimacy. I had not thought about it, but the kind of lost intimacy Kundera was lamenting was what Frank and I shared with our letters. Intimacy has been further eroded in today's times. When I stop for coffee some place I see all these people gathered together, only they aren't really together and they aren't sharing anything. They are mostly all glued to their computers or smartphones. And that is the problem with public spaces today. We don't create intimacies; we share proximities.

Why journey out to a public place only to do what is done much better in private? Why not be public in a public place? It's a real loss of humanness that we do more texting than talking with one another.

* * * *

In July my third child was born. It was a difficult pregnancy for my wife and a stressful time for both of us. There were issues that we struggled with and we ended up on opposite sides of them. However, when our beautiful and healthy daughter was born, it became an opportunity to move forward again. I could not have been more proud to have another child—another beautiful and precious little girl. It also meant a delay of one additional year until the reunion for Frank and I—a delay, but for a wonderful reason.

> **December 1996**
> Dear Stuart,
> Meanwhile I got your letter, thank you so much for it, and for the nice photo of you and the new family member. I hope all is well and she feel good on earth. That is the difference between you and me. I read books about childs and you have childs. But I still have not given up.
> …

I had on occasion over the years dropped hints about Frank's family background. Of course, my uncanvassed question was always the elephant in the room: *Frank, what did your father do in the war?*

I think I could have asked at this point. He would have been upfront and honest. But I didn't feel it was right to ask. In that letter, he unexpectedly digressed in some detail:

> …Did I ever told you that my mother came from East Prussia? They lived there in a little village, today it is not far from the Russian–Polish border. We were there once in 1970, as I was a child but I remember something. My grandfather was a member of the cavalry of the land-police. He died 1944 from stomach cancer, with age of 55. The family lost all in the war, the last house in a little village burned out. In this time at the end of the war, at the beginning of 1945 my mother (she was 21) had to do what they called an anti-aircraft helper in Koenigsberg (today Kaliningrad) and sometimes she told from the bombardment of Koenigsberg (it was totally

destroyed in few nights) before they took flight from the front. Sometimes she dreamed of it many years later. After the flight they met with her mother and her sister in a little city in Thuringia which in this first time was a part of the American sector.

Recently we visited Schlesien (today the southwest of Poland), the homeland of my father, with him, his sister and cousin and my brother to let us show the places where they were born and have lived and let us told some of the old stories. It were for me really emotional moving days. In the last three years, since my mother was died, I am more interested in the history and the past of my own family. Sometimes I've had the unclear feeling that I miss a real homeland.

I was born and grown up in a little city, where my parents came eight years before in 1952. I think such things are not all the same, but of course it is not necessary to be or to become lucky. But as we were there at the places where the family of my father had lived I had to realize that my connection to the land is only a historical and something like a wish to feel the old roots. In fact it is mostly an emotion inside of me, which has not more much to do with the concrete old places and these land there. It is the wish to be accessory to or a part of a more concrete homeland which carry all the history and which give you a abstract kind of safety. It was sad to realize that it is not more to find there and it is lost for our family forever and I can find safety only inside of me and with my people here, which of course is an other thing and necessary for everyone.

...

Frank continued on about a very controversial book, *Hitler's Willing Executioners* by Jonah David Goldhagen. It created an international sensation when it was published for asserting the average German's complicity in the Holocaust.

> *...For me, much more near was the discussion around the book of Mr. Goldhagen. His book has found here, of course, a very big consideration and I follow the discussion with great attention. My father was born in 1923 and visit school in the time of fascism and came to the army in 1942. We often spoke about that things and as he does experienced it.*
>
> *For me it is this time of German history really not far away. Particular in consequence of the End of the GDR and the Reunification the great problem of fascism and the Holocaust became again very actual. After the war there were two German histories, it mean two different ways to try to accomplish what is happen in fascism and that means the process is not finished and now we need a joint, a common process. And of course the GDR was a dictatorship, too; a moderate, but a dictatorship.*
>
> *I am still out of work, but that is not a problem because I didn't search from I decide to become a private psychotherapist. And in May—I think you already know what will come now—we plan to come to Canada, may be for three weeks. What do you say now? In fact, we would like to come to Toronto, it means to you if it would be possible.*
>
> *I'm looking forward to hear from you. For this time I'll end here. All the best wishes for you and*

your family and your "east German" (geographically we still live in the east) friend.
Your friend,
Frank

That was the first time Frank mentioned anything about the war directly. He mentioned his mother's and grandfather's experiences, but not any details about his father. I admit I found this a bit curious. Frank and I had been friends for years now, but in all that time I had not yet had the nerve to ask him point blank what had been on my mind from day one.

Did he know what I was wondering? And was he reluctant to tell me what his father did in the war because of nefarious details he was too ashamed or fearful of sharing with me?

Deep down I really believed that, one way or another, it would make no difference. I had long before settled in my mind that Frank was free of any connection to the past. However, I was still wary of Germans in general. Did I really believe that, or had I simply made an exception for Frank—and for different reasons, my lovely German au pair?

Frank expressed interest in visiting me in Toronto, and by then the timing was right for all of us. I was really looking forward to it. I had not fully appreciated just how much and I hadn't inculcated what our relationship meant for me, or what sustained our implausible friendship for so many years.

February 27, 1997
Dear Stuart,
Today I got your second letter. I have to excuse me. Already some times I thought to write you but then I delay it again.
Really it is not easy to believe that we will see us after such a long time. It began with one short

afternoon together in former East Berlin. And till today I don't know for certain how it comes along to extend over 14 years. Sure you wouldn't find much cases as we are one. After all the years it could be, in spite of the letters, that we will see one the other really as the first time. So in fact I'm really curious about see you in person and understand what was the thread between us over all the years, the deeper meaning of our letter-connection. Do you have an idea?

...

That there cannot be many cases such as ours is an eminently plausible hypothesis. Did I have any idea why our friendship had managed to span—at this point—fourteen years? I had many ideas. But one of them—as the balance of his letter exemplified—was that he was among the kindest and most open-minded and least judgmental men I had ever known. He began by telling me about a museum he had visited with (curiously) his father—a museum that he would escort me to many years in the future.

> *...One was the new Jewish Museum which they arrange in the renovated New Synagogue. It was very interesting and I've learned much about former Jewish life in Berlin and the Jewish parish today. ...Recently at the psychoanalytic institute where I have my psychoanalytic education we have read the Moses texts of S. Freud. He has wrote two about Moses: "The Moses of Michelangelo" (1914), about a sculpture in Rome which shows Moses with the code of law and "The man Moses and the monotheistic religion" (1939). It was very interesting and a good opportunity to engage with early Jewish history. And it was amazing for me to see how present the early*

history of your daily religious life is, particular that you read about Moses in Torah on every Sabbath and read the Torah one time every year.

...

While our families and many of our friends—secular Jews—could not accept the decision to enter into a deeply religious life, here there was, a native German East Berliner extolling the virtues of daily religious life and of the annual cycle of reading the Torah no less. Truth be told, at this new stage of my life it was *I* that was less accepting, finding I had less in common with those with whom I once had shared values and purpose.

I had no such obstacle with Frank, who unreservedly expressed his support towards me. And in the most wonderful way: by being authentically happy for me; by being genuinely curious and open-minded about my choices. I paused for a long time over that letter, and wondered how in the world I would ever express my thanks to him—my gratitude. His pending visit was so exciting and the anticipation for his arrival was building daily.

We all look for answers. And often we find them in the most unexpected places. Or in the most unexpected people as I would continue to discover in extraordinary fashion in the years to come.

April 4, 1997
Dear Stuart,
Thank you for your last letter. We fly by Canadian Airlines, "what else"? It is very kind that you will pick us up from the airport, and there it is so early in the morning we have our whole day before us.

What shall I tell you? Now where the day of our personal east–west reunion comes nearer and nearer, I missed the words and wait also excited for the moment to see you again.

There are two films (movies) which I like very much, both not easy, some times very sad but which I want to recommend you: "Shine," the true story of an Australian pianist which went insane, the main actor got the Oscar. The other is the "English patient" (got some Oscars). I was very positive surprised, that such serious movies got the prize, for me a good sign. But I just ask me, have ever time to go to the movies? Probably not.

Okay, my friend, I'm not in the situation to write a longer letter. I think we should identify one the other. The "countdown" goes. We are at the "point of no return." Till soon good days for you and your family, your friends.

Your friend,
Frank

That July Frank and Kati made the trip to Canada. I went to pick them up at the local airport. It was a surreal experience. You know the feeling when you see someone close to you after such a long absence? And then you are there—suddenly together again. The exhilaration, emotion, a warm embrace, the staring at one another, an introduction to a new partner and then there is the brutal realization of our mortality as the time that has elapsed flashes speedily by and I was twenty-three years old again for a brief moment—but in reality I was thirty-seven. Where did those years go? Was I happy with where I was? So many thoughts mixed with all the excitement were very present inside of me. But boy, was it fantastic to see Frank again.

They stayed with us for a week, deep in the heart of a religious Jewish neighbourhood in suburban Toronto. I know it sounds like a cliché, but it was like we never parted. We fell into what it was like in 1983; only this was better. A deeper, more enriching experience. He was now a free man. Incredible. Fourteen years ago he and the other 16 million East Germans were part of a virtual communist prisoner experiment that thankfully ended not a day too soon. I was very proud to host Frank and Kati in our home. It felt like being back on the kibbutz and receiving mail from East Berlin…but I have to admit, this surpassed it all.

We did some of the commonplace touristy things. We all went to Niagara Falls and for *my* first time went *behind* the Falls—what a site! And we visited the CN Tower. Frank and Kati rented a car and drove up north to see our rugged Canadian wilderness and then returned to our home for a couple more days before their return to Germany. It was a remarkably easy time together. I was a bit nervous that despite all the letters between us, in the fourteen years of this special friendship Frank and I spent a grand total of approximately two hours together prior to this visit. I had wondered if face-to-face would be different this time, easy, or awkward. During his time in Canada Frank and I went out alone one night to a local pub and ended up talking at some length about the reasons behind us staying in touch. The Wall had been down about eight years by then. It was the first time we talked point-blank about our German–Jewish connection and what it symbolized to each of us.

As I pondered the thought I openly and with humility said to him, "I was trying to prove to myself that I could be friends with a German." He understood that. In return, Frank said he was always curious about Jewish people. I was the first Jew he had ever met. Certainly he had met more of us since our first encounter, but I was the only one with whom he shared a close and special bond.

I talked about my background and growing up amongst so many Holocaust survivors, which led to my natural proclivity towards a hatred for what the Germans perpetrated against my people. He didn't seem shocked or even surprised by that.

We joked about how easy and natural it was being together again. I was a tremendous curiosity for him. He was more curious about me as a Jew than he was about trying to prove to himself he could be friends with a Jewish person. He didn't have any of the hate or the mistrust towards my people as I did with the Germans nor did he have any cause for that. And he admitted, he was haunted by overwhelming guilt "for the sins of his fathers." He said many in his generation were—he was not alone holding onto that with heaviness.

I believe he still carries that guilt. He finds living with the thought of how the generations of his parents and grandparents could do what they did, an ongoing burden for him to carry.

His visit was far too short. I didn't want it to end. He took me back to a place and time that I missed. He reminded me of the authentic person that I am. Being with him again was also a difficult reflection of who I was slowly becoming. It wasn't always easy for me to open up with a "guy friend", but even with Frank—I stopped short. For me, at least, the elephant in the room was still the subject of his father.

What did your father do in the war? I just couldn't go there.

I bade farewell to Frank and Kati at the airport and wondered when I would get another chance to broach that barrier once more. Did I think it would take another fourteen years? I am not sure—probably not.

And while I was afraid to raise the subject of his father, Frank was the primary figure in my life that I looked up to as I continued to subconsciously battle with the absence of my own father. His wisdom, worldview, empathy, compassion and guidance are what I was sorely lacking throughout my adult life. And Frank's departure left a void…as he walked through the security checkpoint, time stood still.

I would love to say that the wall between Germans and me was gone—it was not.

Frank was still an anomaly in my life. If I couldn't accept his father's unknown past, then I was still trapped behind it.

And additional, denser layers were forming all around my existing wall.

Frank's departure coincided with my life with the religious community deepening, my worldview narrowing, my old social circle contracting and my adherence to the ultimate power was becoming fortified. Israel was surfacing as the focal point—the lines between love for Israel and religious observance were becoming increasingly obfuscated. Our lives revolved around the kids' Jewish school, community, the religious calendar and synagogue. Even my work life was affected by all of this. Keeping kosher meant not dining with my colleagues and clients. Being Sabbath observant meant leaving work for home early on fall and winter Fridays with sunset occurring in the late afternoon hours. There were the commonly known religious days off work for Rosh Hashana (Jewish New Year's) and Yom Kippur (annual day of atonement and fasting), but additional religious holidays needed to be taken off, as well—many of those that are not too widely familiar, like Shavuot, Sukkot and public fast days—including four days of Passover: two in the beginning and two at the end of the holiday. It was this religiously intense inward focus and attention that emerged into an *Us vs. Them,* an almost self-imposed, ghetto-like mentality. The community was hypersensitive (and perhaps rightly so) to possible anti-Semitic incidents locally and certainly violent attacks anywhere in the world committed against the Jewish people—particularly in Israel.

This is not the place to debate what constitutes anti-Semitic versus anti-Israel attacks; suffice to say that an attack against the Jewish community in Israel elicited frenzied reverberations in Jewish communities throughout the world, not the least of which existed inside religious communities. You see, inside those communities one of the highest religious aspirations (some calling this a biblical commandment) is to move to Israel, to "make *aliyah*."

A majority of people I knew at my synagogue had immediate family either having already moved to Israel; were themselves hoping, if not planning to make the move; or had children temporarily studying there. That was me. It was my dream to make *aliyah*.

After hearing of an attack in Israel, there would be unmitigated fear for the safety of loved ones there. My neighbour was hosting religious services Friday evening, February 2nd 2001, and I sat beside a friend of mine, Michael. Several men approached Michael with a kind glance, an uncharacteristically gentle handshake and a whisper. I didn't dare ask Michael anything, but I turned to a man on the other side of me to inquire. On Thursday evening, February 1st, a car driven by a doctor returning home from work at an Israeli hospital was ambushed by a terrorist and with eleven shots hitting the driver's car, killed Michael's first cousin.[27] Tragically, this was not a one-off story. Within those communities, and I can speak with authority, each time this was met with a reflex of hate-inspired revulsion. The rancid talk of incompatibility between Judaism and Islam or just Islam and the West was openly and loudly expounded.

During the short time after Frank left Toronto there was a period of regular violence in Israel. There were wars in Lebanon and Gaza that brought destruction to many in the region, but it was the Second Intifada that lasted roughly for five years beginning in September 2000 that intensified the intolerance the Jewish people had in the religious diaspora for the Arabs and Muslims. And then there was September 11, 2001. I too felt all that hate and intolerance. I spoke publically many times in synagogue raising funds for Israel. And I wasn't shy about who I felt was our enemy. I wasn't bashful about verbally regurgitating the many horrific attacks against my people to make my case for raising funds for Israel even more forceful.

I cocooned ever more fiercely into the religious community. I began going to synagogue more regularly and this ritual, amongst others, became for me almost an obsession, an escape and a new identity…a new me.

My German wall was a porous one, allowing me to let Frank in as I had. But this formidable and more resilient wall against Arabs, Muslims and the Palestinian people was something different entirely. It was about *today's* enemy. It was today's news. And it was becoming my present day battle.

There weren't many letters after Frank left Canada. I didn't know that at the time, but times had changed.

> ...Particular thanks to your daughter for gave us her room and her bed!
> Coming back home I came immediately in trouble with my working plans and all it still last on, it is terrible and I'm near to going insane about the problems. After all I didn't got the admission or the license to work in a private practice. In Germany it is not free for doctors to become private and open a practice.
> ...

Apparently the German government had decided that there were more than enough private psychotherapists and had refused to license any more in the Berlin area. I thought this was an interesting sign of the times.

> ...As you can imagine this really knocked me off my feeds [feet]. In Berlin the situation is very difficult and it's really heavy to "get a feed [foot] in the door," as we say. [He discusses establishing a practice outside the city.]
> I become more and more a houseman, do all the things at home (cooking, shopping, cleaning and much more things). I only miss the children (!), while Kati every morning goes to work. I can understand more and more how a woman feel, who do not work and stay at home all the time. She started a work in this psychiatric hospital, where I worked a year ago. But she doesn't earn money for her work. She is hoping to get a contract there later. This is the situation here today, really crazy. That's what we have learned in school about capitalism and the

exploitation of workers. In former times, but that is over now, it's an old, and another story, which I want not to tell you now again.

Recently I cooked jam from berries which we harvest in the garden of my father. The best taste you can imagine!

And then I'm envious of all my friends which have work and make their plans. I'm at home now nearly a year and so long I have enjoyed it, but now I have so much plans and energy, that I want to start now—but nevertheless have to wait, a terrible situation.

My father is still very well and I hope he will stay longer in this good condition. In July he becomes 74 and we will have a little party. A week ago he had a class meeting [reunion] *from his college time (he finished school in summer 1942 in a little town, which belong to Poland today). It's amazing that from his class, only boys, which all went into the war then, there are still 12 men alive.*

...

Here and a bit earlier, Frank mentioned only in passing his father and even noted his time in the war, but provided no detail.

…That we have seen us was really very well, now that I have an imagination how you live, about your family and all things around. It is another feeling now to think of you and to write you. I'm sure that it now will not last 14 years again till we see us the second time.

Particular greeting to my little friend [my son], *I wish him good luck and much goals for the next*

soccer game. Greetings also for your two daughters, particular from Kati, and for your both of course, so we are your friend,
    Kati and Frank

It was, in fact, another fourteen years before we would meet again.

CHAPTER 10

RITUALS TAKE HOLD

> You can have no greater or lesser dominion than
> the one over yourself. The greatest deception men
> suffer is from their own opinions.
> —Leonardo da Vinci

I had a dream once that Hitler came to my door. Growing up, I had quite an imagination—so much so I can't always remember what I dreamed of, or what I just imagined. It started with sports and thinking or hoping I would be a hockey star and doing the math determined that I could be playing alongside Bobby Orr (unfortunately, Bobby's knees gave out, as did my very limited talent). I also had convinced myself I would meet and end up marrying Marcia Brady of *The Brady Bunch* TV series. She was my first love.

But then, one day, my imagination took a dramatic (and dark) turn.

Growing up, I was surrounded by neighborhood kids who were children of Holocaust survivors. Many of their parents had heavy Eastern European accents and some with numbered tattoos on their forearms. There was also a sizable Italian community nearby. A nondescript Canadian accent was the rarity back in those days as Toronto, one of the most culturally diverse cities of the world, was (and still is) a city of immigrants.

My understanding of Hitler, what he did, the magnitude, the depravity and sheer evil of him and what he represented was a slow learn for me despite my communal surroundings.

I believed in the possibility that Hitler was not dead. This was when I was still young, before my bar mitzvah for sure. After all, his body was never found. Based on Hitler's year of birth, he could easily have been in his early eighties at the time.

The really bizarre part of the story is that if alive, I imagined there existed the plausibility of him living in Toronto. Paranoia was apparent—as once mentioned to Frank in a letter of reports that the notorious Nazi Joseph Mengele had been living somewhere in Canada.

One day Hitler knocked on my door to our apartment. It was like a scene out of *Casablanca* with me as a pint-sized Humphrey Bogart. "Of all the doors in all the towns in Canada, he had to pick mine."

I opened the door.

I had a baseball bat in my hand. Sometimes it was a hockey stick. The intention would be to beat Hitler to a pulp. I would do what I needed to do.

This went on for a while. Eventually the dreams stopped. I never saw Hitler at my door again. But there would be new enemies at my door.

By 1998 Frank and I wrote fewer and fewer letters to one another as the email age was upon us. It was only a few months since he and Kati visited Canada, which solidified and heightened our relationship, so much so that he jokingly suggested in his next letter that my wife and I acted as surrogates for him and Kati—still without children. Our fourth child arrived with our third still in diapers—resulting in many concurrent and beautiful changes taking place in our home. Our third beautiful daughter was born with an electric smile, an effervescent personality and soon to be adorned with extraordinarily curled brown ringlets of hair.

> *January 15, 1998*
> *Dear Stuart,*
> *Thank you for your letter and the greetings. Also from us the best wishes for 1998, particular that all will be good with your fourth child, that is a real surprise and a challenge for you!*
>
> *Excuse me that I write in this real old-fashioned method* [the letter is hand-written], *yours is not so old-fashioned as this one. I think sometime the world or we lost much if we give up all these old-fashioned things, which make our lives more rich while hold a connection to the past.*
>
> ...

Frank went on to talk about how difficult it had been finding work and that he was still essentially without work. It appeared he needed to requalify (policy remnants of the less-than-perfect German reunification) and the suggestion had been made to apply to a hospital outside of Berlin for further education. He managed instead to take an examination for re-qualification in November and passed, and would receive his license at the end of January. I could certainly sympathize with him on the work issue front.

> ...Thank God, it was really a hard time with all this insecurity. And I have no more money. We spent our last money in ski holiday in Austria.
>
> Do you take it as a sign that She became pregnant when we were with you? We take it as a compliment. Kati got also a job in a hospital, a place I worked some years ago. She started 5 January. Still no time for a child. Could it mean you get a child for us?
>
> I see you are very moved in Middle East politics, and may be you are right with your thoughts. My father visited Israel for ten days in December. He made a trip what here is called a Christmas pilgrimage, with his sister and some other people. They visited all important places there, not only the Christian. He came back very enthusiastic about all the old historic places and the atmosphere. But they had not much contact with the Israelis. But he likes the country. Sure I want to see it.
>
> ...

I think of this time in my life as a semi-lost decade. Stress at work was slowly building and by the end of this ten-year period I was lost and the uncertainly of my work future was turning me inside out. From the outside, however, it all looked great.

I was working for a state-of-the-art international technology company, initially hired as an account manager—it was a good job. For a time I thought my career path had taken a real upward swing, and until 2004 it did and it had. It turned out to be much more than just regular sales and that was a huge relief to me and my ego. No more Willy Loman worries.

I also had a lovely family with a beautiful wife and now four beautiful, healthy children. Years earlier in a letter, Frank had mentioned the simple things in life and the satisfactions they bring. "What more can one want?"

The truth is, children are life's greatest blessing and its greatest joy. And yes, they can be a trial sometimes, as any parent knows. In his spooky intuition, Frank hit a nerve in that letter. He told me to watch my children to understand the meaning of life. He could not have known how right he was. In their later years, I had been doing far too little watching or engaging with them. Instead, more and more my children saw me withdraw or escape at times of stress. I'd often go to the basement alone and work in my office.

It was a repeated theme in my life that I liked or needed to be alone far too much of the time.

They heard frustration in my voice—exasperation. Once, one of my children told me after the fact that I had embarrassed her in front of her friends. I know that a parent is by mere existence an embarrassment to his child's friends. But this was not what one might describe as normal embarrassment. I had behaved badly and—most seriously—I wasn't aware of it. I was becoming so wrapped up in myself I was not really *seeing* them.

Sometimes I would get depressed, I would withdraw and go to my bedroom and just lie down and close my eyes. Occasionally I would lose my temper and slam a door or yell. They would see me short-tempered or rude with their mother. They would not see us being happy together and I did not often show affection.

How could I not have seen what I was doing by withdrawing like that? Just because I was not seeing, didn't mean *they* were not seeing. They saw everything.

My father had left. He was not there. And I hated him for it. But I was doing something almost worse: I was there, but not there.

My wife and I were not getting along. We tried to hide our disagreements, but any couple in this situation with children knows this forced discretion is almost as bad. We weren't fooling anyone. My children were seeing me come home from work and out of the gate looking annoyed and unhappy. Instead of leaving my frustration at the door, I carried it around with me. I would withdraw as usual and decompress from the day. I would not want to talk with anyone.

Years later, one of my kids told me that I regularly looked angry. All the time? *All the time.* So even when I thought I felt perfectly at peace, my face said I was angry. At the dining room table, where the family assembled for the traditional Sabbath meals—Friday night dinner or Saturday lunch—I would many times become upset if the children were misbehaving. It would just be normal fidgety children stuff. It didn't matter. I would snap at them or glare disapprovingly. Did they sense this meant I disapproved of them?

I liked playing games—some of the time. But they would notice how easily I could become frustrated. I would suddenly get up and walk away. I was very competitive and didn't like to lose. I rarely played board games with my wife. Why? I felt she was smarter than I (and rightly so) and I resented her winning.

I would quickly apologize after an outburst, recognizing that I had again behaved badly. What embarrassed me—what embarrasses me to this day—was not controlling myself or filtering my emotions. I know that the kids saw that I wore my emotions on my sleeve—not hiding anything, even my sadness.

I think about my actions constantly—especially in terms of my children and the effects it had. Frank and I wrote often about feeling helpless in the world because we were only one voice. When we know how easy it is to hurt someone close to us—how deep the wound can go—how can we pretend that one voice is irrelevant? It isn't the number of voices that matters; it's what that one critical and prominent voice is saying.

* * * *

Back at work our company was the proverbial new kid on the block chasing very big and complex deals; our biggest competition was IBM—it was David versus Goliath. And I had my slingshot and rock all ready to go. I really wanted to bring them down. (This was early 2000s.)

By this time I was a dedicated account executive positioning and leveraging our company and partners into the pursuit of an outsourcing deal of a lifetime that turned out to be an immensely significant transaction for all involved. I worked on the deal literally day and night for almost three years. It didn't help that I had a toxic relationship with my boss. In fact, a short time before we landed the deal I was put on probation for insubordination! I was incredulous and becoming a wreck.

I hated the rollercoaster ride stress of it. It was a real battle. And not just with the client and doing all the work that needed to be done. I also felt that some of my colleagues—who were supposed to be helping and supporting me—were constantly working behind my back to sabotage me and take over the account themselves.

Luckily, there were two others leading the deal with me. Together the three of us, each with defined roles to play, pursued the deal in symbiotic precision. Finally the client signed a seven-year contract worth several hundred million dollars. It was a milestone for our company that was covered by the financial press.

It was the biggest deal most of us had ever secured; I felt like a minor leaguer who just hit a grand slam in the World Series, or a rookie who scored a hat trick in Game 7 of the Stanley Cup final—I felt triumphant! We had knocked out Goliath! It was beyond my wildest dreams—and beyond anything my father could ever have hoped to accomplish, and it was real and not some bullshit story I made up to make myself look like a giant—this was no fairy tale. We had the signatures in ink. I was so proud. I was also exhausted. As I mentioned, it had been a rollercoaster of huge emotional highs and devastating lows. I was so shattered by the end that when the contracts arrived with the signatures, I remember I broke down and cried. I was spent.

But it was worth it. Or at least, I thought it was. It turned out that according to company rules I had not been properly "goaled" to the project; what that meant was, technically, even though I led the account from start to finish *for more than three years* it was my two colleagues who made out like bandits since they were "working" in and for the outsource division—I was not.

I was frustrated and confused and disappointed. *It was so fucking unfair!* After challenging the system with the support of a sympathetic company executive, I received a discretionary bonus, which I was grateful for. Were it not for him I would have earned nothing on the deal. And not surprisingly, I received no support from my boss…

It had been a very corrosive and emotionally toxic environment at work and though I tried—at least at first—to leave the hazmat suit at work, eventually the poisons leaked out at home. Overall, the whole situation was eating me alive. I was working late every night and taking my frustration home with me—and taking them out on my wife and the children. I am sure I was impossible to live with. Anxious, impatient, short-tempered and cross. Always ready to bite someone's head off for the silliest thing.

I needed out. It had been a familiar pattern in my life to feel unappreciated. I often assumed people were lining up against me—even conspiring against me. I was absolutely consumed with morbid self-pity and annihilating doubt. This confirmed it for me. I was just so tired. I had nothing left. So when an opportunity came to be "packaged out", I raised my hand and negotiated a severance and left.

The next few years were very personally and professionally unsettling. It was a very tough time. I completely lost track of time and as for my letters, even emails to Frank—and his to me—reached a trickling low.

At the same time my volunteer responsibilities were also consuming more and more of my time and attention. Increasingly my mind was ever elsewhere. We had our kids in very expensive Jewish private schools and it was compromising our financial future. The more confused I became in my life, the more I obsessed I became about my—our—orthodoxy. I turned into a barking drill sergeant wearing an imaginary black fedora. If the kids failed to do it right (a religious commandment!) I would bark at them; if they failed to observe it properly or failed to show the requisite respect I would lose patience. In short, if they acted like kids instead of tiny rabbis I would disapprove.

Looking back, probably that whole time I was hiding behind the safety of the rituals and not dealing with a lot of things in my life that mattered. I was assuming a higher community profile with my commitment to volunteering; I was building a profile of the *important man*. It was not a conscious act, but looking back saw myself as important and a man worthy and deserving of respect. It was very hard being in that environment and among so many successful men and women. People of "real" stature. The pressure I put on myself was incredible. The pretending was unbearable.

And of course, all I could think about was that I had—even after all my success—turned into my father after all. I had failed. Again.

It was very important to me that I be seen as a conventional success—that I be looked up to and be admired, especially by my family. What I was not admitting to myself, however, was that I was beginning to feel more and more hollow inside.

I had promised myself that I would not turn out like my father. I would not run out on my family. I would be a good husband and father. I would be a good provider.

The great Jewish religious leader Hillel wrote: "If I am not for myself, who will be? If I am only for myself, who am I?"[28]

Who was I? I wasn't sure. Who was I for? No one.

What was the point of all this? I had not a clue.

* * * *

And none will hear the postman's knock

Without a quickening of the heart.

For who can bear to feel himself forgotten?

—W.H. Auden

Not only had the number of letters with Frank diminished overtime by this point, but also the letters themselves changed. Of course, they weren't actually letters anymore. They were emails.

I thought it a remarkable technology at the time and hardly gave a thought to what it might mean in terms of losses elsewhere. It seemed as though the easier it became to talk to one another, the harder it became to say anything meaningful. At least, that has been true for me. I share Auden's enthusiasm for the heart-quickening joy that attends the arrival of a letter. It was an occasion! It isn't the same now.

Emails exist purely for convenience and immediacy. They are demanding and insistent. "I emailed you three minutes ago! How come you haven't answered?" Even emails these days are too slow.

Emily Dickinson believed a letter represented a kind of tangible "immortality" because "it is the mind alone" without the actual physical presence of the *Other*—the *Thou* in its essence.[29] I like the idea of letters as bridges; as a physical act of a reaching out of *I* to *Thou*—and I know that Frank did, too.

Perhaps writing letters was a richly secular way I had of what Rabbi Sacks called "making meaning."[30] It was a ritual—a process—and a means to an end, even if I was not sure what the end was or what it might look like. I didn't think it mattered. It was the doing that mattered.

I am not sure the orthodox life ever really felt natural to me. It was a lot of forced effort. I needed the rituals; I needed the meaning the rituals created and that I could sustain for myself through constant repetition. In hindsight, the rituals and community gave me a sense of home that had eluded me ever since my father left us.

And I think that was where a lot was going wrong for me. When I first entered the orthodox life, the rituals were a path towards meaning and significance; rituals organized my life and solidified my immersion into the religious community. The rituals weren't the meaning, however. And that changed. I felt like I had spent years repeating tedious finger exercises patiently learning how to play a piano only to realize, with elaborate emptiness, that I had no desire to play music.

The rituals had become the meaning; an end in themselves. At the time, the life of ritual and regulation made me happy. I have heard that the only difference between a rut and a groove is perspective. And it wasn't as if I was blind to the absurdity of much of what I was doing in the eyes of many outside of the religious community.

I remember well June 17, 1994. My wife and I were glued to the TV watching dozens of police cruisers in low speed freeway pursuit of murder suspect O.J. Simpson cowering in the back seat of the infamous white Ford Bronco. It was surreal and sensational, and like almost everyone else in North America we were absolutely riveted to our TVs—until sundown.

Technically speaking, the Sabbath was about to begin and an observant Jew is not permitted to actively use electronics on the Sabbath, such as watching TV. Comically, that presented a huge decision to make. In our baby steps journey towards orthodoxy we had not yet accepted this mantel of observance. However, earlier that week we had arbitrarily chosen Friday night, June 17th, to begin applying that Sabbath stringency to TV watching. Do we keep watching? We debated for quite some time watching as the Shabbat clock ticked down. Finally, we decided we *would* turn off the TV (my insistence, not her's), but then I called my mother on the phone to receive regular O.J. updates. Our Sabbath restriction on the use of the phone had not yet been adopted. Just a few months earlier, I had to compromise on something I had already begun to adopt: going out in a car on Shabbat.

The prohibitions concerning the biblical ordinance of not performing work on the Sabbath can at times appear confusing and contradictory. It is the combination of the word "work" and "fire" that determines what can be done and not done on the Sabbath day. "Six days you shall work and the seventh day is holy to the Lord." Work is also fire. "You shall not kindle a *fire* in any of your dwellings on the Sabbath day." A car engine uses combustion, technically using fire or ignition to propel the car.

The previous October I had been invited by a good friend to attend Game 6 of the World Series between the Toronto Blue Jays and the Philadelphia Phillies. Toronto was up three games to two and with a victory in Game 6 in Toronto, the Blue Jays would win their second of back-to-back World Series titles. I recall being tormented about the time I was to be picked up by my friend—it was still clearly within the time bounds of Shabbat—but not by much. I ended up leaving home early, violating the Sabbath rules, but was privileged to see that famous walk-off World Series winning home run by Joe Carter.

I was reminded of my reaction to the MADE IN WEST GERMANY cutlery. I had to ask myself, how was my reaction to wanting to continue watching TV or attend the baseball game any different? It wasn't, but it should have been. Violating the Sabbath is a biblical matter, the origin of one's cutlery is purely a choice, and not commented on anywhere in biblical or rabbinic rulings.

The real problem was that I created a rationalization that allowed me to pretend I had not compromised my commitment when I had. In other words, I was being incredibly selective in what I chose to observe and what I didn't. But so do many of us. I needn't be so hard on myself—I know that now.

Through it all I tried to maintain a cheerful and buoyant tone I took with Frank, but it was mostly forced. I was feeling absolutely at loose ends. What I noticed as well was that much of the political urgency of our earlier letters had been replaced by more personal details of family life—new and more important priorities.

I don't recall, for instance, even writing to Frank about the September 11 attacks. It's a significant omission especially because inside the Jewish community I was becoming more and more single-mindedly belligerent in my political attitude.

I maintained the appearances of domestic and communal tranquility as much as I could. We made the decision early on that our children would be enrolled in private religious day school, and we paid a hell of a price for that. I wasn't regretting it, not in the least. For the most part we still maintained our orthodox lifestyle both inside and outside the home. But things were snowballing out of control. I found that overtime I was taking on more and more personal stringencies of religious observance. I was asked to join a committee at our kids' school. I was throwing myself in as many extracurricular responsibilities as I could. I eventually took leadership positions there and spoke at the synagogue raising funds for Israel. I really enjoyed the work. I thought it was important; but I realize, too, that it strongly fed my ego. One committee led to yet another, and another. In 2006 I was elected president of the school board. It was a lot of work and I spent a lot of evenings away from home on board business. And when I was home there were endless phone calls and emails to deal with. It was unceasing and all-consuming.

After a couple of job failures I took a contract position in the Jewish community thinking that since I loved volunteering in it, why not work in it? I was becoming reasonably well known for my political engagements, some of which were covered in the Jewish dailies. I was indirectly involved in the Ontario provincial election in 2007 under the banner of fair funding for faith-based schools. Let's just say that didn't end too well.

I was a motivated and vigorous public speaker and enjoyed it. We raised tens of thousands of dollars for Israel Bonds and Israeli ambulances requiring replacement after many were destroyed during the Intifada. I took the writing of my speeches very seriously and rehearsed them for hours and hours so that they appeared off the cuff, but weren't. (Aside from hearing of this technique from reading a biography of Winston Churchill, it turns out that many of his wittiest and most spontaneous remarks were premeditated and rehearsed—I first learned this trick myself in high school.) There would be hundreds in the audience during my speeches. I had a very theatrical and emotional delivery style—they were *with* me on the journey. I persuaded them to arrive to the understanding and belief that there were only two kinds of people out there: *us* and *them*. *Only we* (Jews) *can take care of ourselves. They won't help. It's up to us. Look to your right and to your left. These are the only people you can trust. No one else.*

Help them hate the enemy. It was a very simple, but effective strategy. And I was very good at it; I loved performing. But I believed in what I was doing, too; I had no doubts about my truth. It was up to *us*. *They* were out to destroy us.

The truth is never that simple. Certainly mine wasn't. Not then.

There was one remarkably memorable evening. I was one of a number of honourees at a school fundraising dinner in recognition of all past board presidents and a key benefactor. It was a prestigious event. I felt triumphant. I appeared on top of the world. I remember being among all those extravagantly successful colleagues, friends, and associates while wondering if they could see what I saw.

I was a fraud.

I was unemployed. I had no immediate job prospects. My career was in ruins. I was at my lowest ebb in terms of self-esteem and self-worth. My marriage was on the rocks and I was having profound doubts about my commitment to my faith.

I was becoming more and more like my father.

CHAPTER 11

MY EARTHQUAKE

> People should worry less about what they do and
> more about who they are.
> —Meister Eckhart

From: Stuart Lewis
Date: Mon., Aug. 23, 2010 at 10:52 AM
Subject: Berlin travel plans
Hello Frank, just a quick note before I confirm my travel plans for January.

I am looking at a flight that gets me into Berlin on Monday Jan 24, 2011 early morning. I can visit some sites in Berlin while you work, and I can meet you at your home in the evening—perhaps drop off my bags somewhere, your home or your office. I see that I will arrive after your 51st birthday, so we will have to have a drink together and celebrate being the same age (I turn 52 in June). I will fly to Manchester, England on Thursday morning, Jan 27. So let me know if this is okay with you. I cannot wait!!

Your friend,
Stuart

> *From: Stuart Lewis*
> *Date: Thurs., Dec. 23, 2010 at 6:55 PM*
> *Subject: Berlin travel plans*
>
> *Dear Frank:*
>
> *I cannot wait to see you in a month's time.*
>
> *I am going to Washington, D.C. tomorrow with the kids. I was in contact again yesterday with our American friend Hank—we will meet for the first time in 27 1/2 years on Sunday!! That should be a lot of fun. […] After all, had I not met Hank in the train station in West Berlin it is very likely that you and I would have never met.*
>
> *Okay, must run, hope you are well. Look forward to hearing back from you soon. And is the snow melting yet??? Quite the Canadian winter you guys are having.*
>
> *Your friend,*
> *Stuart*

I had spoken with Hank a few weeks before our visit to D.C. He was shocked, but elated that I had successfully tracked him down after all these years. Early in the conversation Hank voluntarily disclosed that he was gay. As Jerry Seinfeld comically performed on his self-named show two decades ago, I, too, said, "Really, not that there's anything wrong with that." Hank and I were reliving our memorable East Berlin experiences, yet it was remarkable how there were particular elements of the trip I had forgotten about. Like our room. We shared one. There was only one bed—and to be as frugal as possible we had to share that, too. Hank finally shared one last fact. Back in Berlin he found me attractive. When I told the family this story they all howled with laughter.

> From: Frank
> Date: Tue., Jan. 11, 2011 at 5:07 PM
> Subject: Only two weeks
>
> Dear Stuart,
>
> The day we will meet again comes more near, only two weeks more.
>
> Thank you for your postcard. Excuse that I didn't answer earlier. But you will see that I have really much to carry out with all this house things. And we have to move with the praxis at the End of March. Our private move will be later, may be in May.
>
> So I hope all is also well with you and the family.
>
> Have my best wishes, I'm really excited to see you and looking forward.
>
> Your friend,
> Frank

It was almost twenty-eight years from my first visit to Berlin. I made my second in January 2011.

Was it a coincidence? I was looking for an opportunity to go back to Berlin and see Frank. Coincidentally, my dear cousin was planning her son's bar mitzvah in Manchester and it was always a dream of mine to attend a family celebration in the UK. I figured that was a perfect pretext for visiting Berlin. It wasn't necessarily an easy decision as money was very tight at the time, but I was able to apply my frequent flyer points to make the journey to both Berlin and Manchester on the same trip.

Frank's home was in what was originally East Berlin. It was an older but very quaint neighbourhood. While I was there, he was still renovating the very same home he mentioned in his letters about how the East German hierarchy worked. It was a fabulous old place. He was converting it to both a home and a private office for work.

It was just as wonderful with him as it had been fourteen years earlier in Toronto. His two kids really took a liking to me and me to them. The first couple of days we just relaxed, toured a bit, and caught up.

I desperately had to ask him the question and I was ready. The question that had been on my mind for almost three decades. I approached it warily. I kind of went quiet for a bit. We were at the gnarled wooden table in his kitchen. Just the two of us. I think he knew what was coming. I don't know. He didn't seem surprised when I spoke with a serious intention:

"Frank, we really need to be open, I have to ask you." I hesitated. "What did your father do in the war?"

It was such a hard question to ask, I was shaking. The last thing I wanted was to offend. I was prepared for anything. I was pretty sure it wasn't going to matter. Although, I don't know, what if he had said he was the top SS guard at Treblinka?

As I said, he must have sensed it. He just kind of nodded and started talking.

I then asked him whether he had any other family in the war. His uncle, who was two years younger than his father, was killed in action.

His father (who has since passed) was still living at the time, but his mother had passed away a number of years ago.

And after I got my long-awaited answer, that was about it.

We talked some more, mostly about small or inconsequential things. In other words, about life. The day-to-day cares and concerns we all think make us so unique, but really the things we all share in common: children, marriages, work, vacations, hopes, dreams, aspirations, small successes and more numerous failures.

Politics? Not so much. None of that seemed to matter. Not any more.

* * * *

I had honestly wondered what my reaction would be being in Germany again. I was a much different person in 2011 than I was in 1983. For one thing, I was—despite my misgivings—still deeply and observantly orthodox. I not only felt very Jewish, but at times while wearing my kippah I was visibly Jewish. (Not to be glib, but for any Jew with identity problems there is no quicker fix than a trip to Germany.)

My flight from Toronto landed in Frankfurt and then I flew on to Berlin. I had never been to Frankfurt. We deplaned by walking down the mobile stairway to a shuttle bus. We all crammed onto the bus and drove off to the terminal building. Suddenly I became very aware of my fellow passengers and not so surprisingly most were speaking German. A chill ran down my spine. I have talked to Jewish friends who have experienced the same sudden cold terror upon hearing German spoken. *What was I afraid of?* It made no sense.

And, yet…

I was absolutely on guard and palpably uncomfortable. I found myself needing to steel myself to my surroundings. To be honest, it was as if the everyday normality of what was going on around me made my anxiety all the more intense and acute. It was hearing all that German. At one point I realized

I was looking around my fellow passengers for an elderly person and I couldn't find one. I remember thinking, *None of you were in the war. You are all too young. You could not have done anything—you simply were not there.*

I went from the, *I'm cool with you guys,* thought—to their parents. In my head I was thinking, *Sixty-five or seventy years ago, people, it is possible your fathers did some nasty stuff*—I quickly changed that thought, too—*but even so, it wasn't you that did it.*

I had to very deliberately process that insight. And it was just about that time that I had an even more peculiar thought. It came to me like a headline: *I am on a mission.*

I wasn't sure what that meant, and I am not sure even today that I know. But I will never forget it. *I am on a mission.* Finally, we reached the terminal and the doors opened and we trundled off. But I couldn't stop wondering: *What could they have been thinking? The ones on the death trains who looked exactly like me?*

Inside the terminal building, with my EU passport in hand, the customs officer waved me through with hardly a second glance and I boarded my connecting flight to Berlin. After deplaning in Berlin I was feeling pure excitement knowing that in a few moments I would be reunited with Frank. I continued through the airport and found Frank waiting for me at arrivals. It was such a warm welcoming. Within moments of our splendorous rendezvous Frank's primary focus was on fulfilling my kosher dietary requirements for me. The first place he took me was to a kosher bakery. In fact, the *only* legitimate kosher bakery I was aware of in Berlin. I was touched that he had taken such care to make sure I only ate kosher meals or purchased kosher products to take back to his home.

Once at his home I was reacquainted with his lovely wife and met his two adorable children. He suggested he take me on a tour right away. I was tired, but readily agreed. I realized later that first day that Frank had not taken me to any sites that weren't Jewish.

During my stay we visited the extraordinary and emotive Holocaust Memorial in central Berlin. He took me to the famous Fasanenstrasse Synagogue in Berlin that was attacked during Kristallnacht in 1938 and virtually destroyed during an Allied bombing raid in 1943. And for dinner one evening, we went to the Jewish Community Centre for a delicious and fully kosher prepared meal.

I felt at peace. But I was also overcome by a feeling that I can only describe as *weightiness*. I am not sure I can explain it, but I think there are two ways we know things: we either experience something directly or indirectly. I did not experience the Holocaust directly. But even growing up in my secular Jewish neighbourhood in Toronto I had those many friends who had grandparents and relatives who died in the Holocaust. Those survivors are a link to all those who did not survive and to be in their presence is in some way—even indirectly—to *know and to feel*. It is the burden we carry around with us unthinkingly—the weightiness of memory.

To understand and to know are different things. The Jewish people do not have a monopoly on victimhood. There were genocides before the Holocaust and genocides afterward. We cannot pretend that we have not suffered as a people. But so have others. As human beings we all have a natural sympathy for our fellow human beings. But walking with Frank along the streets of Berlin, I was haunted by ghosts that seemed not anecdotal history, but my personal history; *my* ghosts from *my* past and not anyone else's. I felt justified laying claim to a kind of privileged identity.

I am here and they are not. Was that what I meant by being on a mission?

I stayed with Frank and his family for a few days. Just as it had been fourteen years prior, I was not looking forward to departing again. This time it was my turn. Friends like Frank are rare and our bond is almost magical. On the morning of my departure the taxi arrived outside his home. It was very early. Frank and I were saying our goodbyes when he suddenly said, "Wait. Wait! Come. I must show you something!"

Suddenly Frank ran down the street and waved impatiently for me to come and follow him. He was standing and pointing down at the pavement. I looked. It was a small brass plaque. There was a name inscribed on it. Frank explained that the brass plaque he was showing me, which was called Stolpersteine, had been placed all over the streets of Berlin to commemorate the Jewish family who lived opposite in that particular house. It was very dark and they were not easy to discern. But I could see how delighted Frank was to show this to me.

We bid our farewells, hugged, I jumped into the taxi and drove off.

As an orthodox Jew, I was required to pray three times a day: in the morning, afternoon, and evening.

According to that day's sunrise, it was still too early to do my private prayer service at Frank's home. I knew I would have to perform it at the Berlin airport. *Oh boy,* I thought. I discussed this scenario with an orthodox friend of mine before I left for Berlin. His father and mother were concentration camp survivors. So Germany is personal for him—I understand that. He told me that he once had to make an early morning connecting flight via Berlin. For him to stop there even for that brief period was barely palatable to him. I have a lot of Jewish friends to this day who absolutely refuse to set foot in Germany. He decided that instead of seeking out a quiet corner in the Berlin airport lounge he was going to pray out in the open. He put on his *kippah* (yarmulke), *tallit* (prayer shawl), and *tefillin* (phylacteries) and started to pray.

My friend is one of the most gentle and sweet guys I have ever met. But on this occasion he was defiant. "I prayed there," he said, "to show those fuckers that I'm alive and praying right here." I was shocked to hear this tone from him—it was so antithetical to his normal demeanour.

Here I was in the same airport and wondering myself where to pray. Should I just defiantly plunk myself down like my friend and pray as conspicuously as possible? Do I have an obligation as a Jew to prove to "them" that they haven't won? That I am still here?

It felt wrong, just as it felt wrong when I heard my friend vulgarly describe his experience in this very same place. I found myself looking around for a discreet location to pray. This wasn't just a regular weekday morning service for me. I was in Berlin. My intention was that I was doing it for all those who perished in the war, who did not have the privilege and the *mitzvah* (doing a positive commandment) of freely praying in Germany or elsewhere in Europe at the time. It was not the same as what my friend had in mind. I was doing it for those who could not pray anymore, or died trying. For those who could not do it themselves, I was doing it for them. It was an exceedingly meaningful and visibly emotional experience for me. To this day the memory is no less so.

I don't think I comprehended it at the time, but for me that was a subtle but profound turning point. I realized what made me most uncomfortable. It was not being in Germany or being in Berlin or hearing German. No, as awkward and uncomfortable that might have been, that was not the most important thing I remember.

It was my friend using the phrase, "those fuckers." I immediately thought of Frank, and his lovely wife and wonderful two children. They were not the enemy. Nor are the German people.

PART II

THE ENEMY WITHIN

CHAPTER 12

MY WALLS CRUMBLE

> When you think your life is falling apart, it's
> usually falling together in disguise.
> —Charlotte Eriksson

As-Salāmu ʿalayka Dr. Abuelaish—I hope I have that correct.

Dr. Abuelaish, I was deeply moved through your words and your indescribable pain and tragedy your family has suffered, as I heard them told by you on Thursday evening June 14th at the event sponsored by the Bereaved Families of Ontario (BFO)—Toronto. You have taken a courageous journey and such an honourable one as well. I feel you are a special human being.

As I briefly mentioned to you, my story is markedly different from yours, but I too have a quest to end hate in the world. The genesis of my story was a chance meeting I had in an East Berlin outdoor café in June of 1983, a brief stop in my journey while I was spending a year after university travelling through Europe and Israel. There I became friends with a local German, an East Berliner, who at the time was in Medical School, now is a doctor himself. Through our saved letters (dating back to 1983) we are trying to impart our true story and mission to end hate, one person at a time. We are early in our journey, but have mapped out a plan.

I would be honoured by an opportunity as we discussed last night to perhaps meet over coffee to discuss life further. I am often downtown on business and I am sure I would be able to adjust my schedule to a time convenient for you.

Be well and kind regards,
Stuart

From: Stuart Lewis
Sent: Sat., June 16, 2012
To: Izzeldin Abuelaish
Hello Izzeldin. Thank you for your kind reply. I would very much welcome an opportunity to meet with you this week. I am available on Thursday—what time and where is best for you?

Regards,
Stuart

An old friend from university, the executive director of Bereaved Families of Ontario Toronto, was holding her annual general meeting and had scheduled Dr. Izzeldin Abuelaish as the special guest speaker. She contacted me, knowing that I was conservative, pro-Israel and an ardent Zionist, and invited me to attend to listen to the good doctor.

I also had some free time on my hands—my wife and I had recently separated.

I knew of the Gaza Doctor and his book, *I Shall Not Hate*, but was hesitant to have any contact with him. He had a tragic story to tell, but I wasn't sure I wanted to attend, or was ready to and possibly end up feeling sorry for him. He was, at least in my mind at the time, the enemy. *He was one of them.*

And what could I learn from this man that I didn't already know?

She said Dr. Abuelaish's perspective might be a refreshing one for me to hear. (I think what she meant in her wonderfully oblique and diplomatic way was that she had become eye-crossingly weary of my preachy two-dimensional views on that debate, and other right and left issues.)

I balked: I was sure I didn't think I wanted to listen to Dr. Abuelaish. I thought, why would I want to meet this Palestinian man?

The more I thought about it, however, the less hostile I became to being open-minded. What was I afraid of? I had, after all, started down this road with the German people—which was a historical and psychological wall that I had built up. Perhaps it was time to heal myself more broadly, and my current obstacle and intolerance with the Arabs and Muslims was unyielding. Hate and anger had been an issue in my life, and I knew full well that I was not comfortable with the old thoughts—something was still amiss, and in real-time I was seeing a new pathway opening up before my eyes. I sensed this mission advancing me forward.

And nothing was going to change unless I made the first step.

I was profoundly stirred by Izzeldin's speech. I was sicked by hearing him tell the gruesome tragedies he suffered. His unbearable losses and his very public reaction to them were incomprehensible. I shamefully think it was the first time I allowed myself to feel anything for the "enemy". I was standing opposite this brave father and gazing upon a face that had witnessed and experienced immense emotional trauma and knew that somewhere, somehow "we" had been wrong. We had all been approaching "us" and "them" so terribly wrong for decades and centuries before that. It took but the briefest moment for the wall I had worked so hard to build to start breaking down; the *I* and *It* had become *I* and *Thou;* "us" and "them" had become *us.* Just us.

After his talk I introduced myself to him and purchased two copies of his book. He inscribed both, one for me and one for my eldest child. We chatted briefly and made arrangements to meet at a later date at his office in Toronto.

I was fifty-three years old at the time and had achieved a modicum of local notoriety as a politically active Zionist, but I had never met a territory Palestinian person before. With Dr. Izzeldin Abuelaish, I have to say, I started at the top. A couple of weeks later we reconvened, and he told me his story in heartfelt personal terms—more so than I heard in his speech or what I read in his book (I made a point to read his book before our meeting). He described the horror. It was almost too much to bear. In his office were pictures and drawings by his children. It was supremely moving, emotional, tragic and devastating to be in his presence. I felt deeply honoured to spend private time with this man. I was in awe. We embraced and I cried as we said our goodbyes.

In many ways this was a far more difficult test for me than was my issue with Germans. I had my anti-German biases and prejudgments. I knew my history—but I was not a part of that history. Hamas and the Palestinian people were my reality; their existing conflagrations with Israel and the Jews is today's news, not historical narratives. Sadly, "Death to Jews!" is not some slogan from the Third Reich and the blood libel is not yet a relic of the Middle Ages.

So I embraced this man—this Palestinian person; this former *enemy*—and found no compulsion to hate but only held a heartfelt desire for peace and for love of a fellow human being.

In July 2014, riots broke out in Calgary during a protest in support of the Palestinian people and in opposition to the war in Gaza between Hamas and Israel. Similar rallies had been held in many cities around the world, including Paris, Amsterdam, Berlin and elsewhere. Authorities in Paris became so worried about potential violence that they banned further protests. Concerns about a rising tide of anti-Semitism were raised across Europe after several hundred protesters attempted to storm two synagogues during an anti-Israel demonstration, chanting "Death to Jews!" and, "Hitler was right."

One does not have to be Jewish to find this hateful behaviour inexcusable and intolerable. But as a Jew, it might be understandable that I took these threats not only seriously, but also personally. I acknowledge that some might not—but I did.

Certainly it may be different here in Canada than, say, in Europe or in Israel. After all, don't we, as Canadians, think of ourselves as among the most tolerant people in the world? According to witnesses at the Calgary rally, a number of pro-Palestinian supporters became incensed when a rival pro-Israel rally began across the street and some Palestinian supporters began a chant of "Heil Hitler." A Jewish protester claimed he was knocked down by protestors and dragged several feet by an Israeli flag tied around his neck. He said he was also roughed up.

"Maybe a hundred of them decided to cross the street," he told a Calgary Herald reporter. "They came around and swarmed around us saying abusive stuff at us like 'Kill the Jews' and 'Hitler was right.'"[31]

A spokesman for the rally issued an immediate apology, insisted the organizers had nothing to do with this incident and called the violence "regrettable."

I happened to be in Calgary on business about a week after the Calgary riots. Just in time for a counter-demonstration organized by Ezra Levant, the right-wing conservative media personality, billed as an event to "take back the streets."[32]

From my perspective the streets looked fine, but what did I know?

I concluded my business in downtown Calgary by late afternoon and figured I may as well make an appearance and see what my fellow Jews were up to. A fairly large contingent had already assembled in front of City Hall; I noticed, also, a much smaller group of men demonstrating across the street. Maybe six or seven in total—all young adults, and very clearly pro-Palestinian.

I crossed the street to observe more closely what was going on. They were standing behind barricades and a line of Calgary police were separating them from the predominantly Jewish crowd that was quickly gathering opposite. I noticed some were cloaked in Palestinian flags, I also saw a couple wearing a *keffiyeh*, the familiar headdress associated with the Palestinian resistance movement. Anger was etched on their faces and discernable in their tone. The counter-protesters incensed the Jewish protesters and the back-and-forth taunting was at a fever pitch. Each side seemed eager to taunt the other back, although I am not sure who taunted who first.

The fellow who appeared to be the leader could not have been older than twenty-one. He was very fit and muscular. His dark eyes were alight with rage. He was screaming at the crowd of Jewish supporters. The more he screamed, the angrier and boorish he became. He yelled back, "Heil Hitler! Heil Hitler!" as he simultaneously snapped off a smart Nazi salute.

I could hardly believe it. I had never experienced anything like this face-to-face in my life. I was stunned. It was *unreal*. His fellow demonstrators picked up the chant. They leaned across the railings as far as they could, and shot out their arms stiffly in Nazi homage.

Oddly, I was not angry. I could have been enraged like the other Jews who were present, and I would have been entirely justified. What I felt, though, was confusion. And simple wonder of what could possibly have motivated these young men to such a crescendo of pure and undiluted hatred.

And that it was happening *in Calgary*—in diversity-loving Canada!

From the other side of the barricade, my Jewish brethren—a large number of them in business attire possibly having just finished work from the nearby downtown office towers—were themselves screaming and shouting vulgarities.

It was lunacy. I scream at you, and you scream at me. I insult you, and you insult me. What was the point? Who shouted first? Who started it?

Who is right? Who is wrong?

Who cares? You are both wrong. We are all wrong. Insanity, I remembered the quote from Albert Einstein, *is doing the same thing over and over and expecting different results.* I thought about introducing myself to that young ringleader and trying out the quote. What would he do? Would he shout at me that Einstein was a "dirty Jew" and attempt to beat me to a pulp? Or would the shock be too much for him? Would he back down? Would he even see me? As long as I was on one side of the barricade I was "them". But on his side, I was "us". Who belongs and who doesn't?

I wasn't sure. He was so hostile. It would be like trying to reason with a rabid dog.

I decided to move out of direct fire and found a seat on a short cement wall a few metres away. Beside me were two young men and we began to have a conversation about how crazy all this was. They smiled politely. I told them I was just visiting here on business and that I was Jewish, but didn't like these demonstrations. I extended my hand to them and introduced myself.

They each shook my hand; I noticed, however, they did so reluctantly and cautiously.

I asked them how they came to be here.

They looked at each other. "We are friends with the Philistinia," one said in a thick Middle Eastern accent.

I asked if they were students; one said he was in a local college, and the other in university. I asked them where they were from. One from Somalia and the other—the one sitting beside me—was from Syria. The Syrian had spectacularly handsome features. I asked them how they liked studying in Calgary. They both nodded. It was very enjoyable, they said. I asked them if they had been able to do any travelling. They said yes, they went to the Kananaskis area.

"You like the mountains?" I inquired in an affirmative sounding tone. "I love them."

The Syrian's face positively lit up. "I too love the mountains." We talked about how Canada's mountains compared to Syria's. His Somalian friend smiled and said that he found our mountains very big. "Beautiful but *very big*."

"Too big?" I asked jokingly. "What about skiing?"

He put up his hands. "No. Not for me!" he said in frightened sort of way. We all laughed. We spoke some more about the mountains; we talked a bit about life in Canada; about their futures, and what they wanted to do when they matriculated from college and university.

Finally it was time to move on. I noticed the rally had broken up and mostly all that remained were a few stragglers who looked like they had no place better to be. Some police officers lingered in small groups and city workers showed up to carry away the barricades.

I said goodbye to my young friends. We smiled warmly at one another and this time when we shook hands the grip from both of them was deliberate, firm and accompanied with broad warm smiles.

A few weeks later I met Khalil, a Palestinian Canadian; a young man who just graduated from teacher's college and was about to begin his first teaching job in a Muslim private school. We crossed paths at an anti-Israeli rally in Toronto that summer. I was wary and reserved when he approached me, but he was very excited and even passionate to engage in dialogue. He surely wanted to talk politics—especially about the blockade of the Gaza Strip that Israel had imposed in 2007, which was a major Palestinian grievance during that summer war with Israel. I wasn't so sure it was a good idea. Was I ready for this? Anti-Israel? Charges of apartheid directed against the Israelis? What was there to learn, here? I felt that many of those in attendance supported the militants, or as some will label them—terrorists.

I decided I would mostly listen to what Khalil had to say. We actually had an exceptionally civil and cordial discussion, which was a bit surprising considering Khalil's starting point. I am quite sure that Khalil was sincere in his beliefs, but maybe he was hoping for a confrontation. But there is my negative and unwarranted judgment percolating into my thoughts—I am still a work in progress.

My first reaction to Khalil was not unexpected and even anticipated: I nodded inwardly, *I thought so. I knew it. Same old "anti-blockade" rhetoric*.

Instead of challenging him, however, I asked a few clarification questions, nothing aggressive, mostly by way of seeking an elaboration on points he was making. I wanted him to explain what he thought of the blockade from *his perspective*. And something odd happened. The tension that I felt between us relaxed; the clenched-fist defensiveness eased a bit. Khalil seemed genuinely pleased to be able to tell "his side" of the story. Our conversation ended inconclusively. I think he knew that he had not convinced me. And perhaps he was both relieved and surprised that I made no effort to convince or to confront him with an opposing point of view.

We were not friends. Nor were we enemies. It was a start.

I am not so naïve as to think that I had made any lasting contribution to the effort at global peace. For all I know, I made no impression on Khalil, either. But what if I did? Would that not be a good thing? Where do we think peace is ever going to start if not between you and I? We are all Khalil. We are all Izzeldin Abuelaish; we are all Leon Klinghoffer. This was, after all, how Frank and I felt about our relationship.

"It can't go on forever." But it can. And it does.

Most of us like to think of ourselves as tolerant. And we are, for the most part. But what is easy to forget is that one is not merely tolerant but tolerant *of something* or *someone*. It's that last bit that is crucial. Tolerance requires that we put our preconceptions and judgments on hold. It does not mean blind acceptance; it means your truth is not the same as my truth.

What it means is that none of us knows what the truth is.

* * * *

I hadn't randomly attended that rally in Calgary. I did so because of another rally that I was drawn to a week previous in Toronto.

Jewish groups across Ontario were up in arms over a decision by the provincial legislature to allow the annual Al-Quds Day rally on the front lawn of the legislature building, insisting it would "promote hatred because some Muslim organizations involved are virulently anti-Israel."[33] (Al-Quds Day is celebrated on the last Friday of Ramadan and was created in 1979 by Supreme Leader of Iran Ayatollah Khomeini, to show Iranian solidarity with the Palestinian people and to oppose Zionism and the continued existence of Israel.)

The decision to give the rally a "go ahead" came only hours before a report from international news services that at a state-organized Al-Quds Day event in Tehran "thousands of Iranians shouted, 'death to Israel' and were observed carrying coffins decked with pictures of Israeli Prime Minister Benjamin Netanyahu and other Israeli leaders."

President Mahmoud Ahmadinejad of Iran was quoted, saying there was "no place for a Jewish state in the Middle East" and he called for "Muslim unity to foil Western support for Israel." He labeled Israel a "cancerous growth on Palestinian land."[34]

Out of curiosity I decided to drop by the Al-Quds rally at Queen's Park in downtown Toronto. It was a pleasant summer day and was out for a ride on my bike. The grounds were crowded with protesters—pro-Palestinian on one side of the Ontario Legislature grounds, pro-Israeli on the other side, both separated by police barricades. Being an invisible minority, especially in my cycling attire, I was able to walk onto both sides simply observing and listening to the hate I witnessed all around me. There was a no-man's land at the foot of Queen's Park Circle and there stood a statue of Canada's first prime minister, Sir John A. Macdonald that separated the two groups by no more than a few metres.

Not too far from where I was, I saw a group of Jewish protesters chanting *"Sharmuta."* As I was about to learn, it's an extremely vulgar Arabic term for "whore". That vile invective was directed towards a young woman who was backtracking not too far away from me.

Her head was down and I could tell she was very upset. I took a step towards her and asked her if she was okay. She explained what had happened. "I'm Jewish," I said irrelevantly. I felt ashamed and tried to apologize. I wasn't sure what to say.

We started chatting and introduced ourselves. Suzanne was twenty-five, of Lebanese origin and wore a hijab—she was an observant Muslim woman. We continued talking and ended up watching the rest of the demonstration from a distance. The rally was scheduled to move on from Queen's Park and down University Avenue to the United States Consulate there.

There was still a fairly large contingent of pro-Israeli protesters on the grounds of Queen's Park. But the mood seemed to have turned less confrontational and more celebratory. They were playing Israeli music and dancing. Suzanne wanted me to take her onto the "other" side, the side Toronto Police refused her entry earlier for her own safety as she was a visible minority in a very antagonistic and confrontational environment. With my bike and Suzanne, we walked onto the "forbidden" territory. Almost immediately an Israeli woman approached us with a large dog on a leash.

She was scowling at Suzanne and I instantly recognized her heavily laden Hebrew accent. In Hebrew, I not so calmly asked the woman what the problem was.

She looked past me to Suzanne and snarled. "What are *you* doing here? You belong on the other side!" Several young men hastily approached me to find out what was going on, clearly seeing me with a Muslim woman "*invading* their space." Even now I cannot put into words how taken aback I was. *This is our side. You belong on your side.* We were less than an arm's length apart but at that moment I felt separated from her by a million miles. Wasn't it the Jews, after all, that had wandered the world for thousands of years in a kind of permanent exile before the creation of the modern state of Israel? And this woman—this Jewish woman—was telling this lovely young woman beside me where she "belonged" and where she did not belong?

"She's with me," I said.

The woman glared at me with a coldly disapproving look. It was Suzanne, however, who diffused the situation with the Israeli woman, and I managed to calm down those young men. Shockingly, she told me months later that it was this Israeli woman who was leading that vulgar chant preceding our first exchange.

I asked Suzanne if she was hungry and if she wanted to join me for a bite to eat; I walked with her as she retrieved her bike locked behind the Queen's Park Legislature, and we rode together to a quaint little Mexican taco restaurant I liked not too far away. We talked a lot and I paid for lunch. After lunch she insisted on reciprocating, so we walked a short distance to a patisserie; we talked some more over coffee and dessert—her treat. In all, we spent five enlightening hours together that day. *Enlightening*—a word I had not used since my introductory encounter with Frank in East Berlin.

The next day I read in the paper that Toronto Police had launched a hate crime investigation into comments made by the former head of Palestine House who had called for the widespread murder of Israelis.

I thought of Suzanne and our extraordinary time together the day before.

I thought of my friend, Dr. Abuelaish, and his three young daughters and niece killed by an Israeli tank shell. The zero sum equation of retribution. You kill one of mine, I kill four of yours. And on and on. It is an algorithm of senseless hate and annihilation.

When will this hatred and the killing end?

Ultimately, there is no "my side" or "our side". We are all partners on the same one planet. This was evident to me from this encounter. There is no "us" and "them". There is simply *us*.

That irrefutable fact—the fact of our shared humanity and the obligation we have to one another beyond our tribal affiliations—had been brought home to me back in December 2012.

I was signing up for a gym membership and inside the facility there were TV screens throughout, and suddenly all of them were flashing news about a mass shooting in a place I had never heard of called Newtown, Connecticut. It turned out a gunman—a young man in his early twenties—had opened fire at an elementary school killing twenty-six people, including twenty children. When police arrived the gunman, who I choose not to name, killed himself. Indisputably it was an unspeakable and horrifying crime—an incomprehensible act.

I left the gym in a kind of fog. All I could think of was the sheer nonsensical loss of so many young innocent lives and their surviving parents. Nothing can be worse for a parent than losing a child. And to lose a child in such violent and senseless circumstances? Sometimes we fall down a dark deep well from which there is no escape; how would their parents cope?

As usual at that time of my life, I went to synagogue Friday evening. The rabbi and a cluster of men, including me, were talking about the brutal violence earlier that day. That night at the synagogue we were having what is called a Children's Carlebach service; a joyful ceremony where the children participate by dancing around in the centre of the sanctuary.

I realized the kids who were playfully dancing were about the same age as the murdered children. I know you can't stop life. You can't stop kids from dancing *here* because something horrible happened *there*. But it all seemed so wrong. No, not wrong. Helpless. I felt so *helpless*.

During the merriment a friend came up to the group as we were still discussing the tragedy. He had not heard the news. He gasped. "Were there any Jews killed?" he asked in a panic.

I was stunned. Would *that* have made a difference? I repeated his ludicrous statement back at him. My friend is not a bad guy; in fact, he is a very nice and pleasant man. He meant no harm. I know that. It was an impulsive response. Or, maybe it was habit: a mindset that conditions us to privilege "our" losses over the losses of others. Because while we want to say, "No, it doesn't; it makes no difference whether the victims were Jews," at some level we think *yes, it does*.

A philosopher who has meant a great deal to me—and has had a surprisingly relevant impact on my life—is Baruch Spinoza. What attracted me to him first was the man himself. Spinoza was a Jewish man from religiously tolerant Amsterdam who became an outcast. He unwittingly managed to have himself ostracized from his Jewish community for his unorthodox views. The writ of excommunication of 1656 (issued when Spinoza was only 23) was acutely and incandescently harsh:

> Cursed be he by day and cursed be he by night; cursed be he when he lies down, and cursed be he when he rises up; cursed be he when he goes out, and cursed be he when he comes in. The Lord will not spare him; the anger and wrath of the Lord will rage against this man, and bring upon him all the curses which are written in this book, and the Lord will blot out his name from under heaven, and the Lord will separate him to his injury from all the tribes of Israel with all the curses of the Covenant, which are written in the Book of the Law.[35]

His crime? Simplistically perhaps, was *asking too many questions*—too many defiant questions; oh, and in public! And also, making statements far too bold for the times in which he lived, like challenging the nature of God and the relationship of reason to God. And like any modern-day whistleblower knows, being disobedient to authority can be dangerous. After all, isn't it the Talmud that states: "Whoever ponders on four things, it were better for him if he had not come into the world: what is above; what is below, what was before time, and what will be hereafter."

So if you know what's good for you, it's probably best to just keep your doubts to yourself.

It is not hard for me to be immediately drawn to and admire someone capable of inspiring such an orgy of admonition and abuse. I like to imagine Spinoza calmly reading his decree and tossing it aside, sighing into the fire with a "What can you do?" shrug and returning contentedly to his studies. His contrariness—his unbendable iron-like willfulness in the face of conform-or-else orthodoxy—was not a rebellion against belief so much as a commitment to reason. He was not against belief (not really) or even against God (not really, again); he was rather a monogamist for truth; he abhorred complacency and especially dogma that masqueraded as truth. I have an image of the teenaged Baruch—just Baruch and not yet the pariah he would become—at a synagogue service. Like most boys his age, he has been here so often he knows the service by heart. Perhaps his mind wandered. *Odd*, I imagine he would have remarked to himself, gazing at the congregation, *but the men stand apart from the women. Does that seem right? Does that make sense?* His thoughts would break up as a prayer begins, his eyes drooping obediently to the page in front of him. He would hear a murmuring of congregants reciting in unison the exotic but familiar Hebrew words. He'd look left at the other men miming the same words; he'd look to his right. Rows of heads would nod up and down in perfect rhyme. *It's beautiful. But what does it all mean? A means to an end, or an end in itself?*

For Spinoza *reason* was supreme; *reason*—the instrument through which we come to know the how and why of nature—was the path to God. In fact, for Spinoza, nature and God essentially were identical. "Whatsoever is, is in God, and without God nothing can be, or be conceived." It was a shockingly original and dangerously confident statement for anyone to make about the nature of God. No wonder the traditionalist rabbis were shocked! Yet even today, debate continues whether to reverse his centuries-old excommunication.

It did not matter to Spinoza what the truth was, or where it was to be found. Anything that stood in way of the truth was, by his implacable logic, an anathema. What brought the mind closer to the truth was instrumental; what distanced the mind from the truth was not. It was nothing personal, he might say today; it's just business.

"I have made a ceaseless effort," he wrote, "not to ridicule, not to bewail, not to scorn human actions, but to understand them."[36]

If the search for truth and meaning meant upsetting the apple carts around him, well, so be it. He could not control what they thought, so why even try? They would do whatever they wanted to do, no matter what. Better let it be done and be done with it. As Rebecca Goldstein wrote in her book, *Betraying Spinoza,* he lived by two rules: first, "we have no control over anything other than the progress of our own understanding." Second, "care only about that over which we have control." Today one might call that "mindfulness." This was the only way, wrote Goldstein, that Spinoza could avoid "falling victim to the crucifying passions" of superstitious systems of belief and stale orthodoxies.[37]

"I do not know how to teach philosophy," he said, "without becoming a disturber of established religion."[38] The irony of his apostasy was that Spinoza would be shunned twice over: in the Jewish community as a dangerous heretic, and in the world at large as a Jew.

Spinoza paid a high price for his freedom. But he did what he thought was necessary for truth.

My truth was being shattered and replaced. The Jewish orthodox rituals were becoming more like a foreign antibody to me every day. I found new friends in Dr. Abuelaish and Suzanne, who were becoming an incompatible part of me in that world. Coming to inner peace with what that represented and in my journey with Frank led me to the most life-altering part of my journey.

CHAPTER 13

WHAT DID MY FATHER DO IN THE WAR?

> You cannot ask people to coexist by having one side bow their heads and rely on a solution that is only good for the other side. What you can do is stop blaming each other and engage in dialogue with one person at a time. Everyone knows that violence begets violence and breeds more hatred. We need to find our way together.
> —Dr. Izzeldin Abuelaish

Dear friends and family:
Baruch Dayan Emet, [God the trustworthy King]
My father, Roy Lewis, Hersh ben Chaim, passed away yesterday, February 11, 2015. The funeral service will be held on Sunday, February 15th, 4pm at Benjamin's Park Memorial Chapel.
May we all have peace in our hearts individually and amongst all of us collectively.

★ ★ ★ ★

I hated my father.

I thought he was a selfish coward for leaving like he did. I felt cheated that my friends all had fathers, and I didn't (with one major exception). Birthdays with him I don't remember at all.

Memories of my father are most related to hockey; either at my games, or going to see the Toronto Maple Leafs on a couple of occasions and watching games on TV together. One I mentioned earlier was that exhibition game against the New York Rangers.

We were sitting behind the Rangers bench and the trainer gave a puck to me. I think I was eight. That was exciting. I loved playing hockey and pleasing my father with my tough playing style. Toughness, that's all he could relate to. He was at the game when I broke my leg at age thirteen. I recall being in the arena's first-aid room and eyeballing a grapefruit-sized swelling on my lower right leg, several inches above the ankle. I was transported via ambulance to the hospital. I had x-rays taken and was lying on the hospital gurney waiting for the results. The doctor eventually came over to me and told me my leg was broken.

My father looked at me and said, "Yes, I knew it was broken." I didn't, and cried. Why didn't he prepare me?

That was it.

In fact, by the time I saw my father this last time he was a very old man. One day, he started to cry over the past we lost. He mentioned repeatedly how he had paid a big price. I didn't ask him what he meant—I just knew what he implied.

I had never seen my father cry. He was very tough that way; very old school; very British, whatever that means.

I had my bar mitzvah in 1972. It was held at the Pride of Israel, a conservative synagogue. That was the only time the family went to shul; for my parents, the bar mitzvah of their son appeared to me a purely social obligation, like a rite of passage not only for me, but for them, as well. Tick the box and move on. We had a small lunch that day and an adult's party at our apartment that evening. I was lost there. I didn't understand anything that was going on. The guests were drinking and socializing. I had nothing to do with it. I felt like I didn't belong.

Years later, I found out that my father was deeply embarrassed that it was all he could afford.

Maybe that is true. I believe it was all he could afford. What I remember most about my bar mitzvah was how embarrassed I was when he was called up to recite the Hebrew blessings on the Torah, stumbling badly. It was painful and I felt like I wanted to disappear inside myself. I had attended after-school Hebrew classes for two years in preparation. I had taken well to Hebrew and had been quite proud of my ability to read it. I doubt my father looked at the prayer even once before my bar mitzvah day. It was customary for a father to give a speech at the celebration. Maybe he did, but I don't remember.

I missed visits by my dad when I was at university. My mother came once to visit and stayed with me when I lived off campus. She cared deeply and wanted to be there for me, but it seemed out of place. We couldn't hang out and go for drinks with my buddies, as I would envision I would do with my father. He wasn't at my wedding. He wasn't there for the birth of my four children. He missed my son's bris and the baby naming ceremony of my three daughters. He wasn't there for my son's bar mitzvah.

I felt all alone as I was navigating life as a man. I had to make all my own mistakes without benefit of guidance, and maybe—just maybe—I would have made one or two fewer mistakes in my life. And just maybe I would have made more had he been around! So many times I didn't know what the fuck I was doing. I didn't know how to be a parent to teenagers. I hated him for that, most of all.

I felt I had missed a lot. I saw what most of my other friends had, and I envied them for being so fortunate.

* * * *

Growing up I assumed my father was just a regular businessman who had a job like all fathers did. He acted like a big shot at times. He travelled all over the world on business. He would often come home with banners from "exotic" places he had been, and I put them up in my room. I also had a little collection of foreign currency because of these trips.

Looking back now, there were signs that maybe things were not so regular or good financially. What does a kid know? First, we never owned our home. Always rented an apartment. And my parents ended up fighting a lot and mostly about money. My mother was a housewife (which was the norm in those days), had never gone to university, and essentially hadn't any up-to-date workplace skills. So my father was the only breadwinner.

We were good friends with one particularly special family. We were the unofficial members of their extended family. They even insisted my brother and I call the woman's parents Bubbie and Zaidy just as the natural grandchildren would, which is quite extraordinary as I reflect back. They were a wonderful family and they were very good to us. We spent a lot of time with them. But then all that came to a crashing halt years later when my father borrowed money from them for a business venture. The venture (if it even existed) tanked and he never paid them back. Not one dime. After that the families drifted apart, but I stayed in touch. During and after university they employed me at their shop, an upscale boys' clothing store. I will always be grateful for the kindness they showed me.

Back in 1993 Dad had called me out of the blue. He wanted me to sign documents that would put me into his will. My father asked lots of questions about my house, my mortgage, the value of the home, etc. He claimed he had an estate of six million dollars and I needed to authorize some papers for my one-third share. I was skeptical to say the least, but I went to meet him. I wisely hired a lawyer and as advised, I told my father I would need to have the documents reviewed first. He blew his top. He went ballistic. He said that was not possible and grew ever angrier as we debated the matter. I knew I had to quickly leave his apartment. I didn't feel safe.

Often I thought to myself I would be happy if he just died already. In essence, on that day he was finally dead to me. And overtime I poisoned him as a person to my kids. If they ever asked me about him, I would tell them condescendingly how he abandoned our family, never providing a dime of support to their grandmother. That's all I knew and I didn't want to talk about him any more. After that dreadful altercation, I occasionally ran into him while out on errands. Those chance meetings were not pleasant.

After the separation in 2011, we needed to obtain a Jewish divorce decree—a standard practice in such matters called a *Get*. Once there, my soon-to-be ex and I surprisingly discovered that the rabbinic court (a panel of three senior community rabbis) demanded to contact both our fathers (after determining they were alive) in order to validate one part of the Get process. One of the rabbis asked for my father's phone number—I didn't exactly have it handy. At that point I had not spoken with my father for about fifteen years. I had to call my sister in Australia (3 a.m. her time) to retrieve his phone number that I was quite certain she possessed. She did. I passed along the number as requested. The call was placed immediately. Though the rabbi who placed the call to my father was sitting in front of us, I could obviously hear only half of the conversation.

Just as the Get proceeding had completed, the rabbi who placed that call asked to speak with me privately. We walked out into the hallway. He told me my father wanted to deliver a message, which would include an apology for past wrongs. This was turning out to be a pretty heavy day! I thanked him and promised I would call to respond. The Get was in March. Nearing the end of the month I still had not called. I knew I had to, but I was dreading it.

I was envisioning what it would be like. The last time I spoke with my father at length had been the major blowout demanding I sign the fictitious inheritance papers. He was so angry when I refused he swore he would donate his entire fortune to Sick Kids Hospital. Leave it to my father to attempt a swindle and when exposed threaten me with a disinheritance using cancer-stricken children as collateral on the threat.

What *chutzpah!*

With the last "discussion" still a formidable memory, I had decided I would call, but there was absolutely no way I would meet him. *Tell me what you have to say. And that's it.* I felt physically ill when I was dialing his number (okay, touching an iPhone keypad) and my palms were sweaty. I had a queasy, sick feeling in stomach—so nauseous I thought I might puke.

He answered. "It's Stuart," I said. I didn't call him Dad. I didn't ask after him. No pleasantries or endearments. "I understand you have something to say to me."

He asked me, "Who's that guy—who called and what's going on?" He meant the rabbi. I said it didn't matter and repeated that I understood he had something he wanted to speak with me about. He said it had to be face-to-face. I said no.

"Let's start on the phone." Nope, face-to-face. It's face-to-face or nothing, he demanded tersely. I repeated my steadfast position, as did he. I said in an exasperated tone, *fine*, and we both hung up not knowing who got the satisfaction of hanging up first. I was so mad. I knew I was being a prick, but I also deeply resented his presumption. Who did he think he was after all this time to tell me how it had to be?

That was it.

I called a close friend to share what had just transpired. We talked for hours about it. I knew I had to call him again. "Not yet," she said. "When you're ready, call him."

Six months passed. In the meantime I met my friend Suzanne. Her friendship made a monumental difference in my life, as it had with Dr. Abuelaish. I had long since fully come to terms with Germans, the significance of Frank's friendship and his ongoing support was something I treasured to keep me going. I had begun to put my life back together and I was pleased with how it was turning out. It wasn't perfect, not by a long shot. But most of my anger and hate was gone and I was gaining newfound contentment in my life. I was practising yoga and learning how to cope with life's stresses through mindfulness and regular exercise. And for the past several years, my work, too, had become a pleasure.

I hadn't yet connected the dots to my father. That was still the overhanging, unresolved, unpacked baggage remaining in my life. One day I realized I was tired burning up so much energy hating him—this was yet my greatest unconquered challenge. What was the point of all this choreographed bickering and ritualized resentment? How would resenting my father change the past? The past was over; it was the present and future that mattered. Once again the wisdom of Spinoza comes to mind: stressing over the past that cannot be changed is wasted effort.

I hardened my position and my father retaliated. I fired at him and he fired back. How was I any different from the guy behind the barricade hollering "Heil Hitler"? I thought of how I reached out to Suzanne; it seemed so natural. And she was a complete stranger. I thought of Dr. Abuelaish and how I broke through my wall of viewing him and others like him as my enemy. And of course I thought of Frank and the many miles I travelled with him. And there was this person who was *my father*, my flesh and blood.

When does it end?

In June 2014 I moved. One of the first things I did was put a small sticky note on the refrigerator door. It read:

When I am ready...my father.

Every day the words on that note met my eyes. Then, on September 15th those words finally penetrated into my soul. I looked at the note and thought about *everything*. I was ready. I had waited long enough; he was an old man. After all, how much longer would I still have the chance?

I called my father that evening. No one answered. I noticed, however, that I was not nervous at all. I called again the following morning and he answered.

"I'm sorry about the last call. I want to maybe make a fresh start."

"I would like that."

We made arrangements to meet two days later.

I read a story about thieves who stole da Vinci's *Mona Lisa* from the Louvre, which I have seen there. What surprised me wasn't the theft itself, but its aftermath. When news broke that this iconic painting—arguably the most famous painting of all time—had been stolen, thousands of Parisians lined up for miles for a chance to walk past the small square on the wall where the painting had hung for years.

Its absence was almost as much of a draw as its presence. That seemed very odd to me.

And yet, that was very much what I felt about my father. In my case, of course, the "painting" had not been stolen, but had simply up and walked out on its own.

Having approached something on the order of reconciliation after forty-two long years, however, I honestly was not sure if (or how) I wanted my father in my life anymore. It was enough that I had made the effort and had reconciled on my terms. I did not need to forgive my father; I had no intention of forgiving my father. I needed only to let go of all that anger and bitterness and hostility. It had to go. And it had to start immediately. I will never forget the day I just decided, *enough*. I had carried him around with me for so long that I had forgotten what a burden he was. And what a burden that was to anyone around me.

I had said *"never"* to my father.

Never is a long time.

* * * *

It was baby steps at first.

A coffee here, a dinner there. Phone calls to see how my day was going and me calling him, as well. It was certainly surreal on a couple of occasions to have back-to-back missed calls and voicemail messages show up on my phone—from my father and from my mother—a secret at the time I felt I had to keep to protect her. I also had Rosh Hashanah (Jewish New Year's) cards displayed on my mantle at home, one from each of them. It all seemed to be happening too fast. And I knew that maybe it was not how it was "supposed" to be. But more than forty years of building walls between my father and I could not be reversed so quickly.

I was okay with building a bridge, just not a very big bridge.

I realized that I was not accustomed to having a father after all the years without one, and not so sure I even wanted one. *How was I to act? Should I give him kisses hello or goodbye, on one or the other cheek or any time I see him? Should I shake his hand?* I didn't know what to do. *And how should I address him?*

Of course, this father of mine was an old man. It wasn't like I expected we would play catch or attend any hockey games together with his hip as bad as it was. It wouldn't be like old times. There had not been many "old times". There was just whatever we had and maybe that was enough.

In December he entered the hospital and was in and out repeatedly until early January 2015. His lungs had filled up with fluid and he was having increasing trouble breathing. I visited him mostly every day I was in town, and we chatted about this and that. We weren't buddies by a long shot, but we were connecting. There had been a major thaw.

Early February his wife of many years, Helen, called from the hospital to say he was having more difficulties. After quickly wrapping up some work I headed over. It was rush hour and the traffic was backed up and it took me more than an hour to arrive for the relatively short drive to the hospital.

Helen was sitting by his bed. The doctors had been unsuccessful in eradicating the fluid build-up in his lungs, she said. He was struggling to breathe. Helen was very worried—I was quite certain the end was near.

He was only able to take short, panting breaths; it looked so grim. When he saw me in my suit and tie, he commented on how "smart" I looked. I stayed for a few hours and his breathing seemed to ease a bit. He saw how tired I looked and suggested I go home and get some rest. So I told him I would leave to go home.

When he left I was fourteen and he was forty-three. When he came back he was eighty-four and I was fifty-five. He was lying in a hospital bed, helpless for the most part. I didn't know what to do. I was no longer a kid; I was certainly not that fourteen-year-old-kid he left behind. I had my own lifetime's worth of experiences behind me by then, a sizeable percentage of which was consumed often more subconsciously than consciously, in dealing with him and what he did, and also what he failed to do. Then he and I were there, finally together again. *What do I do?*

I knew I should have felt a sense of belonging—a father and son bond; I was forcing it, to an extent. I was not sure what that bond was, but I was hoping that it would develop organically.

The next day when I returned to the hospital, I was wearing a T-shirt under my jacket and when I took it off to sit he commented approvingly on my physique.

"You look like a Marine. I'm proud of you."

I was puzzled. What the hell was he talking about? Where did that come from? A Marine?

I remember once being in the bathroom when my father was shaving. I was just shy of eight years old. He said he had volunteered to fight for the Israeli Army. There was a war raging for Israel's very survival and he wanted to be a soldier in it.

This would have been the famous Six-Day War of June 1967. I had no idea what was going on between the Israelis and the Arabs at that time. It meant nothing to me.

Of course, no one knew it would last only six days so my father never got the chance to serve there.

Outside of his hospital room I told Helen what he said about me being a Marine. She smiled. "Well, he should know." I gave her a look that said, "What are you talking about?"

"Your father never told you?"

* * * *

The next day at the hospital Helen said my father wanted to talk to me about something important. I went into his room. In his hands was an old green beret.

I had no idea what this meant. My father told me he was a Royal Marine, Green Beret Commando, Special Ops, a soldier in the Korean War.

I was dumbstruck—my father, an elite commando? To be honest, he was still spinning fairy tales about the millions of dollars he had stashed away over the years that I would soon be inheriting. I had no idea what to believe. So I did a bit of research and I found rather quickly a picture of him on the Internet, in Korea lined up with the other soldiers getting their food. This time he was clearly telling the truth. WOW! My father was part of an elite and highly decorated squad of Royal Marines who served in the 4 1 Independent Commando (read as FOUR ONE—NOT forty-one as I learned).

When he first told me, I wasn't dismissive at all. The shocked look on my face was genuine. Whether it was a lie or the truth, I think my face must have looked the same. I returned the next day, proudly displaying the photo I had found of him. He was touched. He was so pleased that I brought it to him. My father asked me if I wanted to put the beret on. I demurred. I tried it on.

"No," he said. "You don't have it right. Here." He took the beret and put it on himself. "See. Like this."

In the days ahead we talked much of his service. He said he saw many of his brothers killed. And he killed enemy soldiers, too. But he never thought of them as enemies. It was what he had been trained to do. He mentioned one incident in particular when he was caught in a surprise attack on his position by an enemy soldier. Since they were in such close quarters Dad couldn't draw his guns, so they fought to the death with daggers. He said he could smell the garlic on his breath. *"I knew what he had for lunch."*

And he said with such remorse what a young man he was. Now, this was deeply distressing to him.

Killing was a job he and his fellow commandos had been trained to do; it was necessary. He said he wasn't lucky that he survived the one-on-one combat; he had just received better training than the unfortunate enemy soldier who faced him. You can't think about the enemy as a person, he said, with a family or a girlfriend or wife or parents back home. Empathy gets you killed. It's *Us vs. Them.*

* * * *

Occasionally, his placid stoicism deserted him.

On a few occasions while telling me a war story, he would suddenly flinch or grimace. His face would twitch or his right arm would suddenly thrust outward—as if he still wielded the dagger. I heard that story of that Chinese soldier he killed several more times over. This was his first flashback I witnessed.

The most chilling story was to come. It was a time when the 4 1 Independent Commando were under heavy enemy assault. As a commando unit, they were customarily doing the attacking behind enemy lines—hit and retreat, hit and retreat—but the Chinese were ferociously bombarding their position. An RPG barrage struck them. The radioman, crouched not far from my father, was hit. Hit bad. Both legs had been blown off. At this point my father could hardly speak. I thought he might have been choking. But he was lost in his tormented memory. Another flashback. "Did I do the right thing?" he beseeched me.

"Dad, what are you saying?"

He was suffering. Did I do the right thing?

He started bawling. He was crying like a baby. I had never seen my father cry like that. Never. And never is such a very long time.

I started to cry, too.

I have no doubt that my father suffered from Post Traumatic Stress Disorder (PTSD). What I am not sure about is how much of that can explain his erratic behaviour over the years. A large part of me probably wants something else to blame other than him and the free choices he made.

He had been forced to leave active duty after a grenade exploded close to his head and he lost the hearing in one ear. I realized that when my father volunteered to fight for the Israeli army he would have been thirty-seven years old. Being a soldier—having been a commando—had been the best thing he had ever done. Maybe the only good thing.

One day in the hospital I told him I was very proud of him for his military service—I meant it. He looked up to me, tears in his eyes and said, "I am so pleased you can be proud of something I did in my life, son."

He asked me once if I wanted to keep his beret.

I objected. "It wouldn't be right," I said. "It's not part of the code." It was a solemn duty of any commando to never relinquish his beret. My father smiled happily. It was a matter of honour.

He seemed shocked that I knew that. And pleased. Very pleased, whether that is true or not.

* * * *

He was alert, but very weak. His face looked hollowed out and his arms were thin.

My very dear friend Kevin called me that night at the hospital. He told me that next to seeing the birth of a child, being there for the passing of a parent is the most gripping and moving experience possible.

"Stuart, stay there, don't leave."

I did stay with him through the night—with Helen. Staying up all night was not easy. A hospital is a strange place at night. I tried to get comfortable positioning the chairs in his room, but to no avail. That morning I found the doctor and had a candid conversation with him.

He was blunt. "It won't be long."

When I relayed the news to Helen, she was devastated. She was in her seventies and had known my father for forty years. When we came back to Dad's room, he asked what the doctor had told us.

We both smiled pluckily. He would have none of it. "Am I buying the farm?" he bellowed. A nurse came in with another dose of morphine but he was beyond drugs. He kept ripping off his oxygen mask—he was so uncomfortable. Helen kept replacing it, begging him to leave it on.

He let his arms fall exasperatedly to his side. He looked at Helen. *I can't keep fighting. It's okay. I'm ready.* So was I—yet again.

He removed his mask. This time she knew not to fight him any longer. He stopped struggling. He was looking at Helen. She sat on his bed on one side of him and I was on the other. She held one hand, I the other. I watched his chest and it was hardly moving. I felt for his pulse. The doctor said it might be surprisingly strong at the end. It was. I didn't let go.

I leaned into my father, resting my head on his and gave him one last kiss.

"I love you, Daddy," I whispered.

CHAPTER 14

THE WAR HERO

> We have to continue to learn. We have to be open. And we have to be ready to release our knowledge in order to come to a higher understanding of reality.
> —Thich Nhat Hanh

I did not forgive him, especially for what he put my mother through. And I will never forgive him. I accepted him for what he was and what was—the impermanence of a life travelled. For the longest time the only perspective I had of my father was as a father. And in the end that said a lot more about my expectations and me than it did about him.

Don't get me wrong. My father was no saint. Far from it. His failings, however, were not my responsibility. At long last I acquired peace and closure from this tormented portion of my life. Knowing how close I came to never receiving this gift makes it all the more exceptional.

He knew all too well he had been both a bad husband and a bad father. And not just to my family and to myself, but to his other family, as well; to my sister Tracey and her mother Lydia. Tracey entered my life in 2010 (at age thirty-one) and what a blessing that has been.

I have finally accepted my father—the good and the bad. I think of my own children and what they will think of me when my time comes. Will I be missed? Will I have made a difference? Will I have been loved? Or as Adam Smith asked, did I make myself worthy of love?

What will I have *meant?* What will have been my meaning? Was I in fact even on a mission?

My father's time for meaning is over. I hope he finds eternal peace.

Life is full of mysteries; it can be a banal cliché. For me, the mystery that was my father was a literal fact. It still is. For more than forty years and perhaps for my entire life while he was home, my father was a complete mystery to me. He also left emptiness and a void in my life that I worked very hard to paper over and forget.

I never could.

Not long after my father's death I came across another cache of letters, those between he and I—my second batch of letters as a real-time window into my past thoughts. They cover the time my father left us, and supposedly was on business in Asia.

Still, I don't know what the whole truth is about my father. First, I am not sure it really matters. Second, I have put, at the very least, the anger and the bitterness behind me. *I am not him.* I am me.

That was a monumental wall in my life that I was only recently able to break down.

And what about all the "whys" and mystery surrounding this?

I don't know.

The *whys* don't seem to matter. Not anymore. When my father left us in 1974, was it ever his intention to return as he repeatedly promised in his letters? For the longest time I wanted to believe he would. But he never did. Did he ever make a big score in Asia as he said? Had he really put everything on the line to take care of his family? I don't know. I *do* know that my mother suffered greatly because of him. Did he love my brother and I as much as he said in those letters? I hope so. Maybe. There were plenty of times when I wondered.

I choose to remember him as a valiant soldier and a father who did the best he could.

To me, at least, my father was a hero. I have his beret to prove it.

EPILOGUE

WHO IS THE REAL ENEMY?

> You cannot become who you want to be until
> you have changed who you used to be.
> —Orrin Woodward

The truth is, I didn't share nearly as much with anyone else as I did with Frank. Frank was an anchor for me. The safety and relative anonymity of a letter encouraged a greater degree of intimacy on my part. True confession, after all—the written word often is encouraged by a certain formal distance. We unburden ourselves rather easily to strangers, but find it difficult to speak authentically to loved ones. I suppose it's a fear of judgment.

Even when I disagreed with him, Frank forced me from my complacent mindset. Even when I wasn't aware of it (which, sadly, was way too often) he was always a reminder that what I heard or saw or read was *a* perspective and *only* a perspective. A perspective is not the truth. It is only my truth…or your truth.

Only later would I discover the problems I had with *meaning*—of understanding and being understood. Both verbal and nonverbal interactions can be a wall, too. I never made anything resembling the same effort in my own marriage, much to my regret. In my self-absorption and detachment I cut myself off and often didn't allow her in. I made it so hard for her to climb over the wall I had built between us. I take responsibility for that.

Believing oneself to be standing on solid ground (as I tended to believe I was) only to realize you are actually quite far out on a very narrow branch can be disorienting and discouraging. One of the consequences of ritual I would come to understand is that endless repetition can create a white noise deafness to a different or dissenting perspective.

The most important friendship in my life has been with a German who grew up in Communist East Berlin with rudimentary English skills who had never met a Jew, and with whom I had absolutely nothing in common—except for what really mattered.

Rather, it is funny what we think we all have in common. Is it language that creates the frame, or proximity? Is it age or gender or background? Religious identity or political sympathies? Maybe what binds us most passionately to one another are not the most obvious things—not the most proximate things. Language can be learned and barriers can be bridged; assimilation blends together what was once in isolation. Boundaries—geographical or cultural or ideological or political—are just lines drawn in the sand.

We see differences where we want them to be.

Dismantling the walls that we have built—walls that we build every day, whether we think about it or not—isn't easy. It does not happen all at once. It is an effort that can only be done brick by brick. One by one. It requires less passionate reaction and more compassionate reflection, humility and gratitude for what one already has. It requires challenging our most cherished biases, habits and presumptions. Everything we think we know about the world.

We are meaning-making beings. It is up to us. Now. Today.

I finally removed that note stuck on my refrigerator door. The one I put there the day I first realized I needed to resolve the bitterness and estrangement with my father. It was a simple message. It read: *"When I am ready…"*

It's time for the *re-making* of meaning to begin.

AFTERWORD

DENOUEMENT

What I thought was going to be the last letter I ever wrote to my father.

> *February 14, 1978*
> *Dear Dad,*
> *I hope this letter finds you well. I got this address of yours from the letter you sent to Mom's lawyer. I must say we were very shocked that you would even find the ad in the Chinese paper, let alone answering it.*
> *I'm quite grown up now, in case you lost touch I'm almost nineteen. I'll be going to university this coming September.*
> *This isn't going to be one of those letters that I used to send. Like I said, I've grown up and I finally think that I understand the rather difficult situation.*
> *I haven't heard from you in almost two years, and it's been four or five years since you left, I can't remember.*
> *I think that you want to forget about your life that you used to have here. If that is so, I would really*

appreciate you letting me know. At least then I could stop wondering.

I would imagine that you have a family over there, and that could be the reason for you wanting to forget about us.

Hopefully, one day, I would like to come over and sit down with you and have a good long talk, if you want.

Because no matter what you've done, or what has happened, you will always be my father, and I love you for that.

If this is the last correspondence between us, take care of yourself and have a good life.

Love,
Stuart

POSTSCRIPT

A FRIENDSHIP BEYOND BORDERS

by Frank-Andreas Horzetzky, Berlin
Translation from German by Jonathan Styles, Berlin

July 12, 2015

> *You may say I'm a dreamer, but I'm not the only one.*
> —John Lennon, *Imagine*

Behind the Iron Curtain we were glad of any contact that allowed us to communicate across the otherwise impervious border, leading us out, at least in thought, by means of a conversation or a letter. A part of us Easterners always yearned for the West and for the big wide world beyond. It began in childhood with stamp collecting, when we would all compete over who had the most stamps from the most exotic countries. Fortunately for me, I had three aunts in the West who travelled a great deal and who sent us postcards from all over, resulting in three albums which I had proudly filled with stamps from more than one hundred countries. Every so often I browsed through them and tried to picture South Africa, Vietnam, India, or Mexico. And my imagination was led further on by the adventure stories of Karl May, Jack London, R.L. Stevenson, and Jules Verne: *Around the World in 80 Days*—that was my dream. The expeditions of Thor Heyerdahl especially impressed me: the *Kon-Tiki* and the *Ra*—what I would have given to be on board! But a little sadness would inevitably follow such thoughts because, even as a child, and even if I didn't yet comprehend why, I understood that I would never reach these destinations. I was born in early 1960 in the north of Brandenburg, more precisely in the small town of Zehdenick on the Havel river, one and a half years before the construction of the Wall on 13 August 1961. My parents had come in 1950 to this small working-class town as vocational school teachers. All around were woods and waterways, but there was little by way of civilization, just a cinema, an arts centre, and a youth club. And of course that era's great purveyor of culture, the television, which back then consisted of precisely four channels, two each from West and East Germany. The West German television programs, in particular, kept us up to date with what was happening in the world. But as children we nevertheless remained unclear as to what exactly this "wall" was that everyone spoke of. I always wondered to myself, what could be so special about a wall? It began to seem mysterious and sometimes threatening. But it was always present, and remained on my mind long before I first saw it or could begin to guess what kind of border it was that ran through and divided Germany. I still remember how strange it was, at the end of the summer holiday, to bring our relatives visiting from the West to the border control at Friedrichstraße train station. One particular office for those emigrating often had a queue of people waiting with their East German relatives. My parents were always oddly nervous. And then adults would suddenly begin crying as they said their goodbyes. Most of the time it would be the women, my mother or my aunts, too, which unnerved me. Something was wrong, but I did not dare to ask why they were so upset. The office had locally been dubbed the Tränenpalast, the "palace of tears". Later, when I was living in Berlin myself, I would get so used to the border that I barely noticed it. This was the pathology of the (historical) normality in which we were then living. As a student I would often use the Stadtbahn in north Berlin. This ran at one point between the border walls and allowed me to observe for myself our "antifascist barricade", as the ideologues of the GDR called it. I never felt protected, but rather imprisoned and excluded from the world beyond. This sometimes fanned a quiet rage. *Idiots,* I would think briefly to myself, before turning back to my reading. West Berlin, so close but so unreachable, aroused a longing that I would swiftly stifle.

Young students from all over the world often visited East Berlin to take a look behind the Iron Curtain for a day. What does Communism look like? How do its people live? They had likely already heard so many contradictory views. I once met two students from the USA, whom I then joined again a few months later in Budapest. They had brought a book for me, *Child of the Revolution* by Wolfgang Leonhard, a splendid analysis of the situation in the Soviet Union following the October Revolution, the Comintern, and the first years of the GDR after the war. It was a real eye-opener, but eventually I lost contact with the students. Then came a sunny afternoon in June 1983. I was a medical student at that time, in the third year of my studies at the Charité, the hospital affiliated to Humboldt University. A fellow student and I had come from a microbiology practical and seated ourselves at a café on Unter den Linden. Three men our own age were at the neighbouring table. We made eye contact, a few words were spoken, and soon we were sitting at their table and talking. Later, we took a walk together along Unter den Linden to Alexanderplatz. Quite early on my attention was focused on the young Canadian man, who had seemed likeable from the outset. Our conversation soon honed in on the political situation between East and West. This was in the time of the Cold War, and I remember how amazed Stuart was about how well informed we were about the West, much more so than they were about the East, in fact. Receiving television from both East and West Germany gave us a certain advantage in staying informed. Stuart also spoke of his travels and the search for his Jewish identity: he was on his way to Israel to learn of his roots. I remember him telling me that he had not been brought up in a religious household, but was on the verge of turning to faith. This particularly impressed me, as I was myself seeking orientation in the world. Communism was no longer a utopia I could believe in. I envied Stuart's freedom to travel. But he also told me of people amongst the Jewish community where he lived who had lost relatives in the Holocaust. The fact that he was a Jew stirred my curiosity. Few Jewish people lived in East Berlin at that time, and he was the first Jewish person I had met personally. Not far from where I then lived in Prenzlauer Berg, was the sole-functioning East Berlin Synagogue in Rykestraße. Since it is in the midst of a dense complex of old buildings, it survived the attacks of Kristallnacht. Until that point my only encounter with the Jews was in history books as victims of the Holocaust. Antifascism was the state doctrine in the GDR. German guilt for the Second World War and the Holocaust was almost always present. This was the situation in which I grew up, and the responsibility cast a shadow over us during my childhood and youth. The theme was ever present and still characterizes me to this day. And finally, the GDR was a country occupied by the Soviets and this was always perceivable. Right next to my home town in the middle of the large forest area of the Schorfheide was one of the largest Russian barracks, with several thousand soldiers, its own railway connection, and an airfield. We only occasionally saw the soldiers when they drove with their military vehicles through the town to buy or sell something, or when a military manoeuvre was carried out. Private contact with the German population was strictly forbidden, and there were only occasional meetings with our "brothers in arms" on national holidays and on Liberation Day on 8 May. As a child, the Russian soldiers seemed a little sinister, but that dissipated with time. Russian was the first foreign language taught at school, and soldiers would visit us there. We completed work assignments together, took part in cultural programs, talked, and played football against each other. Thus I grew curious about the mighty Soviet Union. Years later as a student, I would make some lengthy journeys through the USSR, which were always great adventures.

The Second World War and its consequences has always accompanied me: at school, in the many books I read at that time, in films, during my travels, and through my parents. As a youth I had been on school trips to visit the concentration camps at Sachsenhausen, Ravensbrück, and Buchenwald. I had their images before my eyes, without ever letting them to get too close to me. Those sights were too cruel and unreal. As a teenager, I observed them without being able to empathize. It left me with a feeling of oppression that I have never forgotten. I had once gladly accepted the East German reading of history, that we lived in a land of labourers and farm workers in a country run by Communists, who had fought against National

Socialism during the Third Reich, had sat in the camps and prisons, and who thus carried less guilt. The particular responsibility of the Germans had always been made clear to us. "Never again" was a commonly used phrase, and we were at least convinced of this. We lived in what was apparently the better part of Germany, where, unlike in West Germany, denazification had been genuine and we had learned from the terrible events of history. We gladly turned a blind eye to the fact that East Germans had held as equal a share in National Socialism as those in the West.

By the time I met Stuart, however, I had already outgrown this naïve belief. And now a Jewish man stood face-to-face with me; a young, likeable man, with whom a personal connection had at once been made. But I had remained naïve in another way, for it didnt occur to me that in Stuart's eyes I, as a German and as a Communist citizen, was to some degree both an enemy and an opponent. He was not only amiable towards me, but also critical, and perhaps I was all the more impressed by his friendliness and interest because of this. He approached me openly and seemed impartial, not making any reproaches. Our short afternoon together ended at Alexanderplatz, where we exchanged addresses and went our separate ways. We had no idea what would become of it. In a diary I kept sporadically back then, I made just a brief remark about this meeting: that I had tried to give a realistic portrayal of life in the GDR. This was very typical behaviour at the time. Among ourselves, we spoke much more critically about the political situation in the East. But in front of Westerners we would defend socialism. It had become clear that we were identified with the system, and students from the West shouldn't be allowed to think that only fools live in the East. My diary entry also recorded

Stuart's parting words: "Keep in touch, Frank." I had a good mind to do just that.

I can recall how this defensiveness felt. On the one hand I didn't identify much with the political system in the GDR and wanted to show that I also thought critically about political events. On the other hand, I lived in this country, had grown up here, and had been shaped by it. That was my home. Here was where my roots were, and where I had spent my childhood and youth. This was a part of me, and I could not view it wholly negatively. One often thinks of dictatorship as a system that permeates and compromises the whole of its citizens' lives. There is no true life within a false life, as Adorno wrote. But this was not how I felt, even if I was nevertheless concerned with personal integrity. The notion that Stuart saw me as a, perhaps even typical, Communist—this was disconcerting. Me, a Communist? I quickly suppressed the idea: no, no, certainly not, I just lived in a communist country. To me it was merely an unlucky coincidence of history that had placed me on this side of the Wall. I could quite as easily have found myself on the other. This was the facetious perspective I gladly took in order to better cope with the irrefutable facts. But to Stuart, I was a German Communist, a rather unfortunate combination in his eyes, even if German Communists had generally not been antisemitic, and many Communist Jews had come to East Germany following the war to build a better country. Our constant struggle with the socialist system, however, stood in opposition to our private lives, in which we felt no different to people anywhere else in the world. We had our families and our friends, we took up a profession. I was studying medicine and wanted simply to be a good doctor, above and beyond any politics. We partied, went to the theatre, and attended jazz concerts. The small matters of everyday life occupied us.

How can I get hold of the new book by John Updike? Or how about those new jazz records? Or I would fall in love with someone and be spending a weekend with them on the Baltic Coast. And when I was unhappily in love, of course, it was the biggest problem in the world. This was how I identified with life in my home town, and it was meaningful.

So to be addressed by Stuart as a German was strange. I was certainly a citizen of the GDR, but had difficulties feeling German. Owing to the legacy of National Socialism and life in Communist Germany, which I also viewed with a critical eye, my sense of national identity was very weak. I just wanted to be seen as a human being, and, even if this contradicted the rhetoric of responsibility in the GDR, the shame for what had happened led me to a fundamental rejection of being German. In this way, I could begin to avert the guilt and embarrassment that I identified with those who had allowed these things to happen, the generation of my parents and grandparents, and was able to protect my relationship with them from these difficult emotions. Because what child does not want to idealize his parents? But the repeated confrontation with this topic by the antifascist tradition in the GDR brought the issue of guilt to the table time and time again. The visits to the concentration camps led inevitably to questions to my parents: What did you know? How did you relate to what happened? How did you deal with it?

At this point I would like to tell you something about my family and its origins. My mother, Brigitta Schiedlowski, was born in 1924 and grew up in the small village of Weisuhnen on the Spitzingsee in East Prussia (today north-east Poland). My grandparents came from a simple farming family. My grandfather, Gottfried Schiedlowski, served as an unofficial officer in the imperial army until the First World War, when he became a member of the Prussian mounted police. He died at just fifty-five years of age in Königsberg in 1944 from the effects of a gastric haemorrhage. My mother graduated as a teacher of household management after school. She served as a young woman during the war at the imperial railway service in Königsberg. During this time she experienced the heavy bombardment of the city, which led to its complete destruction. I still remember how, into the 1970s, she complained repeatedly of nightmares about the bombings. She fled from the approaching Eastern Front in January 1945 together with her mother, Marie-Luise Schiedlowski, who would become an important figurehead for me as a child, and her elder sister by four years, Edith, leading her to East-Prussian family friends in Zeulenroda, Thuringia. By the end of the war my mother was twenty-one years old, and at the end of the 1940s she trained to become a teacher.

My father, Wendelin Horzetzky, was born in 1923 in the small village of Skronskau not far from the German-Polish border. He came from an old Upper-Silesian family of farmers and military officers. My great-grandfather was senior physician in the imperial army and had served in this role in several battles, most recently in the First World War. He died in Starnberg near Munich in 1936. Of his five children, two sons had served as soldiers in the First World War. One of them, my grandfather Heinrich Horzetzky, had graduated as a farmer and was the landlord of various agricultural estates in East Prussia and Silesia. From 1940 he was administrator to an estate in Warthegau, a part of which had belonged to Poland since the First World War, and which the Nazis occupied in 1939. The owner of the estate was a German and "half Jewish", or "Geltungsjude", as the Nazis termed it, called Lehfeld (originally Lewin). After the First World War he had opted for Poland in order to maintain his estate. Being married to an Aryan German, he was spared deportation. My great-grandfather's other son, Henning Horzetzky, one of my father's uncles, studied painting and sculpture in Munich, where he was active as a freelance artist. My great-grandfather's daughters remained unmarried and childless, but were, all three of them, rather progressive for the time, working and thus leading economically independent lives. One was as a nurse, another a dentist in Starnberg near Munich, and the third was a preschool teacher and director of an educational institute for women, providing them with a cultural education in addition to a standard preparation in housekeeping. Aunt Elisabeth, the last mentioned, was the favourite of my father and he spent several school holidays with her in Bavaria. She was progressive in other respects, too, living openly with her female partner. My paternal grandmother, Hedwig Wodarsz, came from the family of an Upper-Silesian sawmill owner. She was the educated woman of the family—culturally engaged, an amateur theatre performer, fluent in French and Polish—and had travelled throughout Europe as a young woman. My grandparents had five children, Brigitte, my father Wendelin, Albrecht, Verena, and Hans.

My father was summoned to military service on 1 July 1942 at the age of nineteen, before he could formally complete his secondary school studies. He then reported to the Luftwaffe, voluntarily, as was then usual. He had learned to glide and developed a love for flying in the Hitler Youth. Thus he arrived in occupied France where he received his basic training, but was not engaged in any fighting, there being no military operations in France at the time. He was then transferred to a motorized unit in Holland for a year. What exactly he was involved in there, besides his employment as an occupying soldier, he never said. It was not until the spring of 1944 that he began his aviation training in Guben, Brandenburg. As a pilot, he was merely deployed for transporting units to Czechoslovakia and Silesia. His most dangerous assignment was to fly senior officers out of Breslau (now Wrocław) when it came under siege. At that time the Luftwaffe had already been largely destroyed, and he was hardly ever required as a pilot. He often later emphasized that his decision to go into the Luftwaffe prevented him from coming earlier to the Eastern Front, and probably saved his life. It was not until April 1945 that he was ordered to Berlin to defend the city. He was fortunate to the extent that he escaped involvement in the fierce battles surrounding Berlin, and that his troops were swiftly dispersed and redeployed to north-west Germany, where he was engaged in conflict with British forces at the beginning of May 1945. That was his story. He would liven up when he spoke of his time in France, Belgium, and Holland: "I was in Paris and in Amsterdam; I have seen the Eiffel Tower, the Moulin Rouge, and Notre Dame." In the GDR, such a claim was indeed something special. Who else could say the same for themselves? The border was closed, no one could reach those places anymore. Yes, when he spoke of those countries, it sounded more as if he had been there on vacation than as part of an occupying force. And it didn't even seem strange to us—no, we even envied him. These were perverse times.

Fleeing the Eastern Front in February 1945, my grandparents left Wartegau with their two daughters and their youngest son, trekking westwards and ending up in a village in Saxony-Anhalt. There, at the end of the war, they maintained a small farm. My father's three-year younger brother, Albrecht, had fallen in battle close to Vienna in late April 1945, at just nineteen years of age. In family stories Albrecht would forever be idealized as an especially talented, clever, and generous brother, whose loss was a particularly heavy weight to carry. And so my elder brother received his name: Albrecht. My grandfather's brother, Henning Horzetzky, had been taken in April 1945 as a Russian prisoner of war at the age of fifty-five, and never returned. My cousin was named after him. My father was released from captivity shortly before Christmas 1945 and returned to his parents. He then became a vocational school teacher before going on to study agriculture in Berlin. As in so many cases, the postwar division of Germany left a rift running not only through the country, but also through our families. Whilst my mother and my father lived with his younger brother in East Germany, my three aunts, one on my mother's side and two on my father's, lived with their families in West Germany. From then on, contact with each other was only possible in a restricted form. They visited us every year in the GDR, as we were not permitted to travel west, and we maintained a constant exchange of letters.

This brief sketch of my origins should illustrate the family circumstances into which I was born fifteen years following the war. It took a long time for me to realize how short a period that was. Today, twenty-seven years after German reunification, and now able to see how much life in the GDR shaped and still occupies us, it is clear to me how much the legacy of National Socialism must still have been present during my childhood, subliminally affecting us. My parents would never have met each other except for the war, so I almost owe my existence to this global catastrophe and its terrible consequences. My parents' families were refugees from the former East German territories. Both families had lost their homes. They, like the greater part of the German population, were traumatized by their experiences of war and the loss of their homeland. They had lost everything and had to manage as refugees in an unfamiliar environment. The theme of homelessness has always been an undercurrent in my family. On the one hand, they accepted the loss of their home country as a just consequence of the Germans' responsibility for the war, on the other it was a source of regret and grief. In 1970, twenty-five years after the end of the war, when I was ten years old and not yet able to appreciate what it meant to my parents, we visited their former home, now in Poland, for the first time. At that time many Germans, including former neighbours and acquaintances of my parents, still lived there. It was a very emotional occasion. I could feel their loss greatly, and a part of that loss thus became mine. I often revisited with my parents, and later took my children and friends there, and in this way built a relationship with my parents' lost home, making it in part my own homeland. At the same time, I was never able to build such a close connection to Zehdenick, the small town in north Brandenburg where I grew up and where my parents never felt quite at home. It was not so difficult for me to leave when, after completing my secondary education, I took up my military service aged eighteen. Subsequently I moved to Berlin to study, and thirty-seven years later, it is here I now feel at home.

My encounter with Stuart also provided me with a reason to talk with my parents about what they knew about the murder of the Jews, what they had experienced and thought. My mother told me that they had heard about the genocide taking place in concentration camps. It had been told of in their village as an unbelievable rumour, which then became a horrific certainty. My father said that he had noticed two Jewish classmates suddenly stop school attendance, and that he had heard about Kristallnacht, and that a Jewish merchant's shop in the small town where he went to school had closed. But it was not something that he had discussed seriously with his parents as a teenager. I assume his parents must have known more about the situation, given my grandfather's Jewish employer who was also a friend of theirs, but that they did not speak about it with their children. My father learned only after the war of the systematic extermination of the Jews in camps. I believed his account, even if it somewhat disappointed me. It could not remedy what had happened or make it any more comprehensible. Somehow I had hoped to learn more, and I wished that they had been more critical of and actively opposed to what went on. But this wasn't the case and we used to argue about it. They were young, naïve, preoccupied with their lives and with the things that concern all young people, and at least to some extent taken in by National Socialist propaganda. In the end, they were what were later called "Mitläufer"—they had been on the bandwagon. How could I not understand that, let alone criticize them? Had I not been the same in the GDR, a Mitläufer, someone who hadn't actively opposed the regime, despite knowing it to be wrong? What became clear to me much later was the fact that my feelings of shame and guilt had been conferred from them. Out of the difficulty of dealing with this arose the fantasy of undoing those horrors. It could not be true, it was too terrible and incomprehensible. Again and again discussion circled around how this could have happened and how we could make sense of it. But we could never truly make sense of it. Despite all our attempts, we never found a satisfactory explanation for the incredible hatred, the willingness to support the destruction of neighbours and fellow citizens, the loss of all human compassion, the participation, the indifference, and the turning a blind eye towards events. Noticing this tendency amongst the German people in the thirties, Wilhelm Reich and Erich Fromm had created the concept of the "authoritarian character". Fromm meant by this a certain pattern of social attitudes, such as prejudice, conformity, obedience to authority, racism, and the rejection of foreign cultures. I read Fromm's *The Anatomy of Human Destructiveness*, and this helped my understanding a little better. But these are theories. For one thing is also clear: as singular as the Holocaust was, the Germans are not so singular in their humanity, even if differences exist between cultures. Clinging on to the terrible reality was something ultimately unexplainable and incomprehensible about ourselves, for we were Germans and belonged amongst those who had done it all. And the constant talk of needing to ensure that we do not allow this to happen again engendered a suspicion in me that some evil could still be within us, in me, ready to break out again. Why else need we be so careful? That caused me some unease. Could I have let myself be seduced, could I have actually done that? It had happened to others. Today I understand that it is contingent on so many historical and social conditions, on family and individual factors, whether a person becomes one of the guilty. I wanted under no circumstances to become one of them. It was hard for me to accept it all, but how could I not feel some responsibility? I think the desire for reparation occupied me for a long time, at first unconsciously, and the wish remained although I had no way of realizing it. This probably explains why I sought a connection with Stuart, besides the feeling that we would get along. There was the impression that here was someone who understood me, that there was a kind of close connection, something familiar, something in common between us. And it was also something special, even exotic, to meet a Jewish Canadian who took an interest in me, a mere East German. I feel honoured to have him as a friend. We shared a desire to understand what had happened and how we could find a way to reconcile the second generation of the victims and perpetrators, and this enabled us, no longer directly involved with the events of the past, to meet each other as normal, free people. Could we each overcome the traumas of our grandparents' and parents' generations? Would it be possible for us to meet on amicable terms?

The letters Stuart and I exchanged helped me to feel more personal responsibility for what had happened. What I had until then only deflected, an abstract sense of shame and guilt, became through genuine human contact a real sense of accountability. Through this personal and open-hearted correspondence, in which Stuart shared with me his thoughts and feelings, the abstract victims of my history books assumed a concrete, living face. In our letters we often talked about our everyday problems, our fears, our loved ones and our children, our political opinions, our conflicts, and our concerns. It always touched me how openly Stuart trusted me and how important my opinion was to him. He accepted and took me seriously in an entirely unexpected way. That always amazed me. How could he, as a Jew, entrust this friendly confidence in me, a German? The letters are a testament to how a fortuitous, chance encounter led to a genuine friendship, one that would have a special influence on both of us.

In what appears a paradoxical way, Stuart helped me to find my missing German identity. It was not until much later that I realized how much I had related my identity as a German to the role of perpetrator against the Jewish victims. They had practically shaped me. It was an astonishing realization that we needed each other. Perpetrators and victims are inextricably linked and will continue to relate to one another following the trauma of their meeting. The scale of the catastrophe has meant, in this case, that the process has continued for generations. My personal encounter with a Jew facilitated the acceptance of my own identity as a German, and as a descendant of the perpetrators. This broke through the feelings of not being German that I had unconsciously used to repel the guilt of my forebears and my own responsibility. Stuart allowed me to reconcile myself with my German origins.

Just a month after our encounter in Berlin on 16 July 1983, Stuart sent me the first message from his journey across Europe. Even in this, his first letter, he wrote in a friendly, familiar tone, as if we had known each other a long time. He rhapsodised on the beautiful girls in Scandinavia, reported on his visits to museums in Amsterdam, and involved me in his consideration over whether Israel wasn't his home country and whether he could live there. He even described our two-hour meeting in East Berlin as "probably the most enlightening hours I've spent in a long time." This surprised me and won me over right away. What kind of guy is this, I asked myself, who could approach me so open-heartedly, so seemingly without fear or prejudice? It naturally engendered my curiosity. I had not been aware, myself, of the importance this meeting would have for us in the future. Stuart had felt it straight away. He had an intuition I still admire and am grateful for. It was the impetus behind our correspondence. Today I would say it was his good will that amazed me. I had unconsciously held the notion that a Jew would be unable to muster such good will after what had happened under the Nazis. Today, I think it was because of Stuart's own wounds, together with a desire to get by any means to the bottom of things, that led not to a retreat, but to his open-hearted character. This not only allowed him to subvert my unconscious fear of incrimination, it also corresponded with my own benevolent mindset towards others.

We hardly knew each other to start with. But it soon became clear to me that I had seen in Stuart much more than a typical representative of the opposite side of the Iron Curtain. The initial defensiveness I had felt at our first encounter, to get along well and, perhaps, to gloss over certain matters, was soon lost once we began corresponding. We confided more, learned more about one another, and became more authentic. It touches me today when I look upon the thick stack of handwritten letters we wrote in the 1980s. This kind of letter writing was a culture of its own. I remembered once again how personal it felt to sit down at night and find more time for reflection and writing, for dialogue. I often created a pleasant atmosphere for myself, put on a jazz record, poured a glass of Hungarian red wine, and smoked a pipe. And to know that this time was being set aside for me, too, all this exuded a seriousness that felt meaningful to me. It was a conversation taking place between us in silence, and in which Stuart was present in my mind. This situation alone, of adjusting myself for longer periods to my counterpart, was a process of convergence that engendered trust. We would appear mentally to each other at certain instances, and the dialogue continued even after the letter had been written. "What would Stuart say about this? I must write to him!" We became important corrective references for each other. Stuart's opinions and perspective on the world carried weight for me. They meant much to me and I realized it must be the same case for him. Sometimes it was so obvious that I wondered what kind of relationship we had formed. It was as if we were external reference points to each other and, importantly, to the world outside. This point of contact represented a third position allowing us to look at ourselves from the perspective of the other. It demanded that we leave behind our stereotypical thinking and to direct it beyond the familiar clichés and boundaries. In any case, I enjoyed it, and appreciated it as a valuable source of happiness.

Stuart came across in his letters as a cosmopolitan, politically interested, highly educated individual. He had a witty way of writing. All of this prompted me to tackle the questions and issues he raised; I wanted to do justice to his sincerity, and not to disappoint him. It touched me that he took me so seriously and was really interested to know what I thought about things. At the same time, he inquired after my studies and my personal life in a warm-hearted way. We sent many postcards to each other from our journeys to various locations. During this period I travelled on several occasions across the entire Eastern bloc: Hungary, Romania, Bulgaria, and especially in the Soviet Union. It always gave me great pleasure as well as a sense of worldliness. And it was always a particular pleasure to find in the letterbox a postcard sent by Stuart from somewhere in the world. It helped me to feel a little less cut off behind the Wall.

A frequent topic of our correspondence was Stuart's active turn towards religion. I hadn't had a religious upbringing, myself, this already being of little interest to my parents. We were baptized, of course, and my East Prussian grandmother prayed with me when she put me to bed. As a child I had religious instruction, but my parents did not attend church on Sundays. This had less to do with the GDR than the fact that they were both non-believers. Religion was pushed to the fringes in the GDR, of course, and at school we learned socialist ethics. So I became an atheist. But a certain spirituality always remained close to my heart, and it was important for me to feel connected with all living things, with my ancestors, and with the world. So it was quite comprehensible to me when Stuart began to seek his Jewish roots in Israel, but I did not associate any religiosity with it. When he began to lean towards orthodox Judaism, I took an interest even whilst the aspect of faith and, above all, the strict ritual practises remained foreign and out of my reach. I never had the impression, though, that he was distancing himself from me or that this was an obstacle to our communication. I knew of Jewish life only from books, by Joseph Roth, Sigmund Freud, Sholem Aleichem, Isaac Bashevis Singer, Isaac Babel, Bruno Schulz, and Stephan Heym, and from Chassidic and Galician stories, all of which could be obtained in the GDR. Somehow it even appealed to me that he was a practising Jew. I had also read the Old Testament, and had been particularly fond of the stories of King David and of Job. I thus had somewhat romantic notions of what it was to follow all these rituals, practised over millennia by so many previous generations of ancestors. I also connected these stories with Stuart. It was wonderful to picture the candles lit for the Sabbath, the Torah being read, and the family meeting afterwards, perhaps with friends, for dinner. I imagine how nice it would be to experience such an evening with Stuart. Obviously I somewhat envied him and his faith, the certainty and security obtained from such rituals, practised for generations. I saw a beautifully laid table before me, with a menorah and Stuart reading aloud, and thought about how we would philosophize together about life and the world. When I visited Stuart with my wife Kati in the spring of 1997 in Toronto, I was somewhat disappointed. He lived with his family in a new house; everything was modern, there was nothing old, and no candlelight. Stuart still looked like someone I could meet in Berlin, beardless, but wearing his kippah and taking care that his food was kosher. In the evening we went to a pub to drink beer as we had in Berlin. Somehow my romantic notions of the Jews had remained stuck in the 19th century. I obviously had some catching up to do...

Stuart and I belong to a second generation, one born after the war. We were raised by parents who had been affected by it firsthand. They passed their experiences, emotions, and attitudes on to us obliquely. Having been directly involved, it was very difficult to share their thoughts and to communicate. They were too traumatized. Our generation, characterized by this transmission across generations, and the subsequent third generation perhaps even more so, is reserved the task of initiating a process of reconciliation. Many young Israelis come to Germany for this reason, and especially to Berlin, completely unconsciously. Somehow we felt this without having reflected upon it at first. The crucial factor, I believe, is that reconciliation requires a real, personal encounter with the other side, that is, an encounter between the descendants of the victims and perpetrators. In my exchanges with Stuart, I realized how much we were related to and dependent on one another. A German of my generation cannot understand his being German, both in the national and cultural sense, without relating to the guilt of the Second World War and the Holocaust. Without my friendship with Stuart, without his critical presence and his alternative perspective of history, it would not have been possible for me to reconcile myself with the past of my forebears and my homeland. And vice versa, Stuart would go on to reconcile himself with the Germans.

Our discussions about Israel and Israeli politics, which were always difficult and particularly controversial, should probably be understood within this context. Given our historical guilt, I always felt intimidated as a German when it came to talking about, let alone criticizing Israeli politics. In the GDR, Israel had been portrayed as part of the imperialist West whilst the Palestinian people and the PLO were regarded as a national liberation movement against imperialist supremacy, similar to the left-wing movement in West Germany. Stuart helped to relieve me of this simplistic view and to take account of the Israeli perspective for once. Guilt for the Holocaust will remain a defining experience in German self-perception for a very long time. To have failed in this way, and to have borne the historical responsibility arising from this guilt, marked a turning point in our historical self-understanding and has thus become a part of our national identity. And likewise, the experience has become a turning point for the Jews and for Israel. This fact will probably bind us, perpetrators and victims, in an unintended, tragic way for a long time to come. And this is what determines German policy with regard to Israel. Both Germans and Israelis are very aware of this. In horror, after the Second World War, at their own unbridled destructiveness, the German population has largely developed a pacifist, or at least an anti-militarist attitude. It no longer felt threatened, lying at the heart of Europe, and it is only in the wake of globalization that a critical view has again begun to be taken. But the situation is much more difficult for the Israelis, whose state is still denied the right to exist by its neighbours. The threat to the Jewish people, from which the Zionists wished to escape by founding its own nation in the ancient Holy Land, is tragic. Whilst I argued that a two-state solution and an end to the settlement policy was the only way to achieve a lasting peace, Stuart defended the corresponding Israeli policy of making no concessions to the Palestinian people. He was worried above all about the Arab states' irrational feelings of being threatened by allegedly aggressive Israeli policy, which was mainly concerned, in fact, with its own defence and with obtaining recognition of its right to exist. I thought that Israel should manage the Palestinian issue not only from its position of strength, but also taking into account its terrible experience of the Holocaust, and that Israel should meet the Palestinian people halfway, even if the Arab world as a whole was hostile to her. But this presupposes reconciliation and mutual tolerance, positions that are too weak on both sides. To continue to refer to who started the conflict, or to historical rights stemming back several thousands of years, does not help at this point. I understood Stuart's one-sided justifications for Israeli policy as an expression of his attachment to Israel and concern for his Jewish roots.

Revisiting our correspondence today, after a gap of thirty years, I realize that we both wrote astonishingly openly and personally from the very start. You would not think that we hardly knew each other yet. But the letters would soon change that. I was very concerned to present my everyday life as atmospherically as possible, my activities at university, how I spent my evenings, where I went to the pub, what books I read, what music I listened to. My letters were often of a private nature, reporting on my travels, or on happy (and unhappy) romantic relationships. Today it surprises me that I didn't write more directly about the worsening political situation in the GDR, which had already become rather agitated. But we of course exchanged opinion on all other kinds of international political events: on Israel, Lebanon, Libya, South Africa, Chernobyl, on the situation in Poland with the Solidarity movement, on dictatorship and poverty in Romania, Bulgaria, and the Soviet Union. Gorbachev's policies of *glasnost* and *perestroika* were always a topic. It is clear that I was initially somewhat pessimistic, as his policies had been criticised in the GDR and similar efforts had not been encouraged there. Later I began to express more hope, but also anger at the rigidity of politics in the GDR. That I didn't write more critically about the situation in the GDR during the early years of our correspondence suggests to me that I myself did not believe there would be change for a long time. I was also totally absorbed in my medical studies, my training as a doctor, and my romantic affairs, that is, with my private life.

On the other hand, life in the GDR was often more political, more so in a certain way that I would feel it to be in the 1990s. The Cold War and the confrontation of the Eastern bloc with the West were always present. In the GDR one's avowal to the communist system was demanded repeatedly. That was true during my school years, and particularly so during my army service and my studies. One was always compelled towards an internal and an external struggle with the system, and was meant to "adopt the party position for our land of labourers and farm workers." As early as my final years of secondary school, in the mid 1970s, we were recruited for membership in the Socialist Unity Party of Germany, the Communist Party. But even then "the Party", as it was simply called, had all but lost its allure and was the object of clandestine mockery. There were many jokes at that time about the desolate condition of the country. The workers themselves, those who should have been supporters of the system, had lost any illusions about communism. As a teenager at school, I had tried to comprehend the communist ideology; there were socio-political training courses, and we read articles by Marx, Engels, and Lenin. The Marxist idea of historical materialism and the fulfillment of the historical mission of the working class to establish and exist in a classless society seemed highly abstract, overstated, and too utopian. But the notion of a fair distribution of acquired material wealth and resources won me over and I have never lost hold of this idea. Each year we celebrated the anniversary of the October Revolution of 1917, and every time it seemed more bizarre in its formulaic rhetoric. Even during my military service, with its regular lessons in politics, the ideological pressure to conform became so absurd that I was finally cured of any efforts to adapt. They also attempted to recruit me as an informal collaborator to the Stasi. When I refused they threatened to prevent me from taking up my place to study medicine. This frightened me, but also confirmed that I had been correct in my rejection of their offer. I was nevertheless able to begin my studies, and it appears they weren't yet willing to go as far as they had threatened. In the GDR, which called itself a "dictatorship of the proletariat", but which always remained a nomenklatura dictatorship (with influential positions being filled by Party appointees), life was always lived between adaptation, collaboration and detraction, more or less resisting. I still enjoy reminiscing how often friends and I would chat through the night, discussing the political situation in the country. What would *glasnost* and *perestroika* look like in the GDR? Hope of improvement in the situation began to take root again. Sometimes friends from West Berlin also joined us. Most of the time we would sit in the kitchen, the air blue with smoke, drinking beer and wine aplenty. How could we bring change? Should one engage politically and how? Should one go to the polls, even if they were a sham, and vote "no"? Was it morally right to apply to leave the GDR and head west, or shouldn't one remain and try to influence the situation here?

The enemies of socialism were, in the GDR and throughout the communist system, an identity-establishing category. Whenever something did not function as intended, the enemy was sought and perceived, and thus the leaders of the GDR blinded themselves to their own mistakes and limitations. We were educated to hate our political enemies. This never worked in my family, but then I was fortunate that my parents did not comply with communist ideology. Half our family, one of my mother's sisters and two of my father's, lived with their families in West Germany and came to visit every year and I was good friends with my cousins. They brought us wonderful collections of sweets, fabulous toys, jeans, and books that couldn't be found in the GDR. Every summer we had a lark together. How could I hate them? Hate and hostility, and their unyielding intensity, have remained alien to me. When we were taught in school about "evil Capitalist enemies" who refused to recognize the signs of the new age, I couldn't believe in it. My relatives weren't exploitative Capitalists, unable to comprehend the world. I felt it could not be true that all those people "on the other side of the Wall" were simply obstinate and hostile. My own experience was different. And yet there was so much hatred in the world—there had to be reasons for this. I often wondered what experiences these people must have had to harbour so much hate. Had I simply been fortunate to escape such experiences as could have caused me to hate? I was often angered, especially by political decisions taken in my country, and disagreed with the ideological narrow-mindedness of our leadership. But hate? If a person stood before me, I saw a human being and would try to understand his motives. And then I could not hate.

The GDR, and Communism as a whole, was a society that lived for the utopian ideal of a better, more just community. I had also been infected with the belief that, somehow, this ideal must be achievable. Doesn't everyone have this desire, this hope within himself? Was it not worth wishing that it might be realized? I still believe today that we humans are driven by this idea, and that it is worth committing oneself to a more equitable distribution of economic gains. The ideals for which well-disposed people all over the world struggle are those of the French Revolution: freedom, equality, and justice.

It has always been about that, even if the course has often been perverted and ultimately failed. In the GDR there was above all a lack of freedom, but also a great deal of equality, and together these often led to a levelling down that became unjust.

What the years after the end of the Cold War showed is that we once again need the utopian idea of a better life. It is not enough, here in our Western democracies, to speak only of freedom, since this has led to ever greater inequality, especially in the form of neoliberal economics, and in no small number of cases to mere chaos. No, the equality and justice that have been completely neglected in the past twenty-five years must also be remembered. Alain Badiou has stated that real political freedom arises only in such social circumstances as to create the possibility of equality. It is all about creating social and political participation for all groups and social strata in society. The European social market economy heads in this direction and I am convinced that we need sensible state regulation to maintain a just balance between the different interest groups, beyond mere economic strength. The social aspect of the market economy needs to be reestablished. It is clear today that rising economic inequality between rich and poor in many Western countries has led to increasing indignation and disillusionment about the creative potential of democracy to ensure more just social relations. The great danger is that this can be exploited by populist demagogues for anti-democratic and nationalist ends. Democracy remains the best form of society and government we know, however exhaustingly complex its practical realization may be.

In the 1980s, when our correspondence began, the political situation had reached the point that people, already so disillusioned, were thinking more and more about how they could leave the GDR. This process had actually already begun in 1976 with the expatriation of the wonderful songwriter Wolf Biermann. This was a definite turning point and many began to follow him. Again and again, friends and acquaintances of mine would suddenly leave for West Germany. I took into consideration the possibility, but wasn't yet at this point. Four women with whom I was befriended, and another good friend, left the country in relatively quick succession. I myself twice made a request to visit relatives in West Germany, which at the time was possible for family celebrations. It was rejected both times because I did not have a family to whom I was likely to return. I did not know at the time what I would do if I received a travel permit. Stuart also invited me to his wedding. What would that have been like, to appear as representative of the Eastern bloc? But this time I didn't even apply to leave, as entry to the West was restricted to visiting direct relatives. The question of emigration was, of course, also on my mind, and I was obviously frightened by how resigned many of my friends were in the face of increased restrictions imposed by the Party in response to Gorbachev's attempt to introduce more open, democratic policies. The fact that, since the GDR's Biermann affair in 1976 and the success of Solidarity in Poland in 1980, we had made steps towards a revolutionary upheaval that was still not apparent to me. There are passages in the letters in which I found myself self-critically reflecting on my lack of political activity. I did not identify with the political system in the GDR, but I was not active in opposing it. The hopelessness and simultaneously unlost hope with which people in the GDR looked forward to change is described in a joke we used to tell ourselves: a boy asks his grandfather, "Granddad, why do you look so attentively out of the window every morning?" "Oh, my little one," he replies, "I'm watching the weather. One fine day all this shit's going to come crashing down." It really wouldn't be much longer in coming.

It was not until autumn 1989, shortly before the Berlin Wall fell, that I attended opposition events organized by the church and participated in demonstrations. The letters from 1983 to 1989 show how my attitude to the social situation in Eastern Europe had become increasingly critical and discontented. On my many journeys through the countries of the Eastern bloc, I had seen again and again how badly the socialist social system was working, how negative the economic situation in these countries was, and the poverty of the people and their cities. We spoke to so many people, and not one of them believed that Communism had a future. They had lost all faith in the Communist utopia—disillusionment had completely set in. This allowed my rejection to become more radical. In a letter from February 1989 I expressed my disappointment and desperation about the country's political stagnation. It was now quite clear to me that we could no longer expect positive change from the political class of the GDR. It only ever enforced more restrictions and its responses to the Soviet Union's and Poland's momentum for change were helplessly paralyzed. The "corrupt geriatrics" of our Communist leadership, as Wolf Biermann had called them, were simply overwhelmed. The dialogue with Stuart, whose reflections were always sensitively put, never in a know-all manner (even though he did sometimes know better), and which were always respectful with regard to my situation in the East—this dialogue helped me to see clearer and more critically the devastating conditions socialism had brought in the East. With his gentle tone, I always felt he appreciated what I chose to write about and discuss. Ultimately, my position changed from one of attempted accommodation to the situation in the GDR, to its critical rejection. This shift is reflected in our correspondence and in the dialogue with Stuart.

The fall of the Berlin Wall and the reunification of Germany, neither of which I had reckoned with, was an overwhelming experience. These were the days and weeks of a new departure and of new possibilities that I shall never forget. My first journeys to the West, to Italy, Amsterdam, and Paris were accompanied by the immense happiness of liberation, a stirring emotion that sometimes still takes hold of me when I am on the road. My letters after the turn of the century show how I struggled with the new, long-yearned-for situation, the emotional and intellectual consequences of changes occurring at a sometimes overwhelming rate. A new world had appeared before us with changed rules and values to understand and assimilate without simply discarding our past in the East. The upheaval was so great, and its psychological consequences so deep, that it still fundamentally occupies me to this day: not least in my profession as a psychoanalyst. Not long after reunification, I completed my specialization in internal medicine before turning to psychotherapy and, in particular, psychoanalysis. The discipline had already occupied me in the GDR where, long suppressed, it had undergone a cautious revival in the 1980s. I could now finally undertake proper psychoanalytic training. Such was the new freedom that I had wished for.

When I've looked with hindsight on my adult years in East Germany, I've sometimes thought that I could have been more courageous. There would have been opportunities for it. Whilst I argued with my parents over their naïve conformity during the War, I failed to notice just how much I had already accommodated myself to the GDR. To a certain extent my parents maintained the inner attitude of two expatriates. They had let themselves be seduced by a dictatorship once and would not allow it to happen again. They neither wanted nor were able to share in the spirit of socialism being built up in the GDR. They focused on their private lives and thus once again became passive adherents, something that was widespread in East Germany and which also coloured my outlook. My parents spent the greater share of their lives under two successive, albeit very different, dictatorships, whose belief, above all, in obedience to authority had existed in Germany since the days of the Empire, and variants of whose mechanisms were active in the GDR. The value of proletarian Internationalism, the brotherhood between the workers around the world, was held in high esteem, even if it would ultimately fade into the background by stages. At the same time, the countries and people of the West were considered with great hostility. We tried to rid ourselves of such an outlook and to think freely, which was difficult enough in itself, for a certain self-censorship was probably always at work during this period. Stuart, helpfully, never reproached me for this. It was no coincidence that the old German folksong, *Thoughts are Free* was particularly popular in the GDR: "Thoughts are free: Who can guess them? They fly along like nocturnal shadows. No person can know them, no hunter can shoot them: Thoughts are free." Some of these freer thoughts found their way into my letters to Stuart. Our correspondence, his stimulating critical reflection on various political developments, in Poland with Solidarity, in the Soviet Union with Gorbachev, or Israel, helped me to deal more critically with my life in the GDR and my attitude to it. For this I am grateful to him.

"I enjoy very much that our contact didn't broke." This I wrote in a letter to Stuart in January 1994. Apparently it hadn't been taken for granted. We were both busy with our everyday duties. The Cold War was over, and the former strife between

East and West went with it. The terrible conflicts of the early 21st century were still to come. Our political discussions had receded to the background, and Stuart had in the meantime become father to two children and was deeply immersed in his religious affairs. I had also finally met the woman with whom I would start a family, and psychoanalysis had now taken possession of me. In an extended sense, we had now arrived at the same point. Our correspondence had aided us both and its purpose, so to speak, had been fulfilled. We could actually have ended our exchange of letters at this point, but it nevertheless continued and today that brings me a particular joy. We had truly become friends.

APPENDICES

APPENDIX A

My passport marked with entry visa into DDR 10 06 and exit 12 06.
I don't know what the 30 90 means.

Berlin Wall, June 10, 1983. I took this picture from a platform in West Berlin overlooking no-mans land separating East from West Berlin.

Frank and I meet in East Berlin June 11, 1983.
The distance between us would eventually become much closer.

Frank (now a free man) and I reunite in Toronto in 1997 for the first
time since we met behind the Iron Curtain.

STUART LEWIS

April 12. 74

My most dear Sons.

I have just about finished my work here in the Far East, it's been a very long journey and a very hard one. I regret with all my heart that I could not write to you sooner but where I was it was impossible for me to write you. This did not mean that I did not think of you both because I think of you all the time and my love for you is very great.

I would like to explain something to you both, and I hope that you will understand I am a type of man who wanted everything for you both and for Mummy, well now I have it but in doing so I lost the things that were most dear to me. It would have been very easy not to have tried so hard, but I had to make sure that, for your future you had every thing.

I will be home about the same time as this letter, but I wanted to tell why

Letter received from Dad where he wrote, "I will be home about the same time as this letter."

Dad attending Remembrance Day ceremony in Toronto circa 2013 proudly wearing his cherished green beret. He clutched onto that beret until he died.

APPENDIX B: REFERENCES

1. Allison Lampert, "French-Canadian man is now sole suspect in Quebec City mosque shooting," *Bangor Daily News,* Wednesday, June 14, 2017, http://bangordailynews.com/2017/01/30/news/world-news/gunmen-kill-6-injure-8-in-attack-on-worshipers-at-quebec-city-mosque/.

2. Dalila-Johari Paul and Jason Hanna, "Vandals damage 100 headstones at Jewish cemetery, polish say," *CNN,* Tuesday, February 21, 2017, http://www.cnn.com/2017/02/21/us/jewish-cemetery-vandalized/.

3. Tonya Maxwell and Tim Smith, "Dylann Roof guilty in Charleston church shooting," *USA Today Network,* December 15, 2016, https://www.usatoday.com/story/news/nation-now/2016/12/15/jury-deliberating-fate-charleston-church-shooter/95474302/.

4. "Canadians appear to be more hateful online. Here's what you can do about it," *CBC News,* January 20, 2017, http://www.cbc.ca/news/canada/marketplace-racism-online-tips-1.3943351.

5. Jonathan Sacks, *The Great Partnership: Science, Religion, and the Search for Meaning* (New York: Schocken Books, 2011).

6. Jonathan Sacks, *The Great Partnership: Science, Religion, and the Search for Meaning*, 2011.

7. Talmud, Sanhedrin, 110a. Retrieved June 14, 2017, http://juchre.org/talmud/sanhedrin/sanhedrin6.htm#110a.

8. Erich Fromm, *Socialist Call* Vol. XXVIII #1, Spring 1960.

9. Erich Fromm, *Socialist Call* Vol. XXXVIII #2, Summer 1960.

10. Michael Cooper, "Protests Greet Metropolitan Opera's Premiere of 'Klinghoffer,'" *The New York Times,* Oct. 20, 2014, https://www.nytimes.com/2014/10/21/arts/music/metropolitan-opera-forges-ahead-on-klinghoffer-in-spite-of-protests.html.

11. "US Bombs Libya," *This Day in History,* April 14, 1986, http://www.history.com/this-day-in-history/u-s-bombs-libya.

12. Adam Smith, The Theory of Moral Sentiments (New York: Cosimo Books, 2011, originally published 1790).

13. Martin Buber, *Ich und Du (I and Thou),* (Martino Publishing, 2010, originally published 1923).

14. Godfrey Hodgson, "Obituary: Barry Goldwater," *Independent,* Friday, May 29, 1998, http://www.independent.co.uk/news/obituaries/obituary-barry-goldwater-1156920.html.

15., 16. Martin Luther King, Jr. and Ali B. Ali-Dinar (Page Editor), "Letter from a Birmingham Jail [King, Jr.]," *African Studies Center—University of Pennsylvania,* April 16, 1963, https://www.africa.upenn.edu/Articles_Gen/Letter_Birmingham.html.

17. Martin Luther King, Jr. and Ali B. Ali-Dinar (Page Editor), "Letter from a Birmingham Jail [King, Jr.]," April 16, 1963.

18. Francis of Assisi, *Goodreads,* Retrieved January 2017, www.goodreads.com/quotes/1149018-start-by-doing-what-is-necessary-then-do-what-is.

19. Erich Fromm, *The Fear of Freedom* (First published United Kingdom: Routledge Classics, 1942).

20. Viktor E. Frankl, *Man's Search For Meaning* (Boston: Beacon Press, 2014, originally published 1946).

21. Erich Fromm, *Looking Backward* (First published in: E. Bellamy, 2000-1887; New York: New American Library, 1960), V-XX.

22. Erich Fromm, *May Man Prevail? An Inquiry into the Facts and Fictions of Foreign Policy* (New York: Doubleday Anchor Books, 1961).

23. Erich Fromm, *On Disobedience: Why Freedom Means Saying "No" to Power* (New York: HarperCollins 2010, originally published 1981).

24. Viktor E. Frankl, *Man's Search For Meaning* (Boston: Beacon Press, 2014, originally published 1946).

25. Jay Nordlinger, "The worst man ever to win the Nobel Peace Prize," *The Times of Israel,* March 31, 2012, http://www.timesofisrael.com/the-worst-man-ever-to-win-the-nobel-peace-prize/.

26. Jonathan Sacks, *Universalizing Particularity* (The Netherlands: Koninklijke Brill NV, 2013).

27. Norman Lebrecht, "Gustav Mahler," *NewStatesman,* May 12, 2011, http://www.newstatesman.com/books/2011/05/mahler-german-eggebrecht.

28. Alan Philps, "Arabs and Jews unite in grief," *The Telegraph,* June 15, 2017, http://www.telegraph.co.uk/news/worldnews/middleeast/israel/1320913/Arabs-and-Jews-unite-in-grief.html.

29. Pirkei Avot, "Ethics of the Fathers, Chapter 1:14," *Chabad.org*, Retrieved June 14, 2017, http://www.chabad.org/library/article_cdo/aid/2165/jewish/Chapter-One.htm.

30. Emily Dickinson, "Emily Dickinson's Letters," *Emily Dickinson Museum*, June 1869, https://www.emilydickinsonmuseum.org/letters.

31. Jonathan Sacks, *The Great Partnership: Science, Religion, and the Search for Meaning* (New York: Schocken Books, 2011), 8.

32. Jen Gerson, "Pro-Gaza protests worldwide tainted by anti-Semitism; Calgary organizer to apologize for violence," *National Post*, July 21, 2014, http://news.nationalpost.com/news/canada/pro-gaza-rallies-worldwide-tainted-by-anti-semitism-calgary-organizer-to-apologize-for-violence.

33. Damien Wood, "Ezra Levant hosts 'Calgary for Israel' rally outside city hall," *Calgary Sun*, Thursday, July 31, 2014, http://www.calgarysun.com/2014/07/31/ezra-levant-hosts-calgary-for-israel-rally-outside-city-hall.

34. Atara Beck, "Toronto's Jewish community braces for al-Quds Day protest," *The Times of Israel*, Thursday, June 15, 2017, http://www.timesofisrael.com/torontos-jewish-community-braces-for-al-quds-day-protest/.

35. Reuters, "No room for Israel in 'new Middle East': Ahmadinejad," *National Post*, August 17, 2012, http://news.nationalpost.com/news/ahmadinejad-israel.

36. "The Text of Spinoza's Excommunication," *Minnesota State University*, June 14, 2017, http://web.mnstate.edu/mouch/spinoza/excomm.html.

37. Baruch Spinoza, *Goodreads,* Retrieved June 14, 2017, https://www.goodreads.com/author/quotes/122092.Baruch_Spinoza.

38. Rebecca Newberger Goldstein, *Betraying Spinoza: The Renegade Jew Who Gave Us Modernity* (New York: Schocken Books, 2009).

39. Baruch Spinoza, "Baruch Spinoza Quotes," *iPerceptive,* Retrieved June 14, 2017, http://iperceptive.com/authors/baruch_spinoza_quotes.html.

ABOUT THE AUTHOR

Stuart Lewis, businessman and writer, lives in Toronto, Canada. His thirst for learning and adventure took him behind the Berlin Wall of East Germany in the spring of 1983— a journey that led to a profound philosophical introspection and (life) transformations decades later. That life began as a secular Jew and evolved to religious observance and ensuing struggles. Ultimately, he allowed the world to become a part of him and he was ready for anything. Stuart hopes this work will prompt others to ponder their own predispositions and ultimately bring down walls in their own lives. His first book, *When Walls Become Bridges* is his compelling and thought provoking story.

www.ingramcontent.com/pod-product-compliance
Lightning Source LLC
Chambersburg PA
CBHW030229100526
44583CB00013BA/632